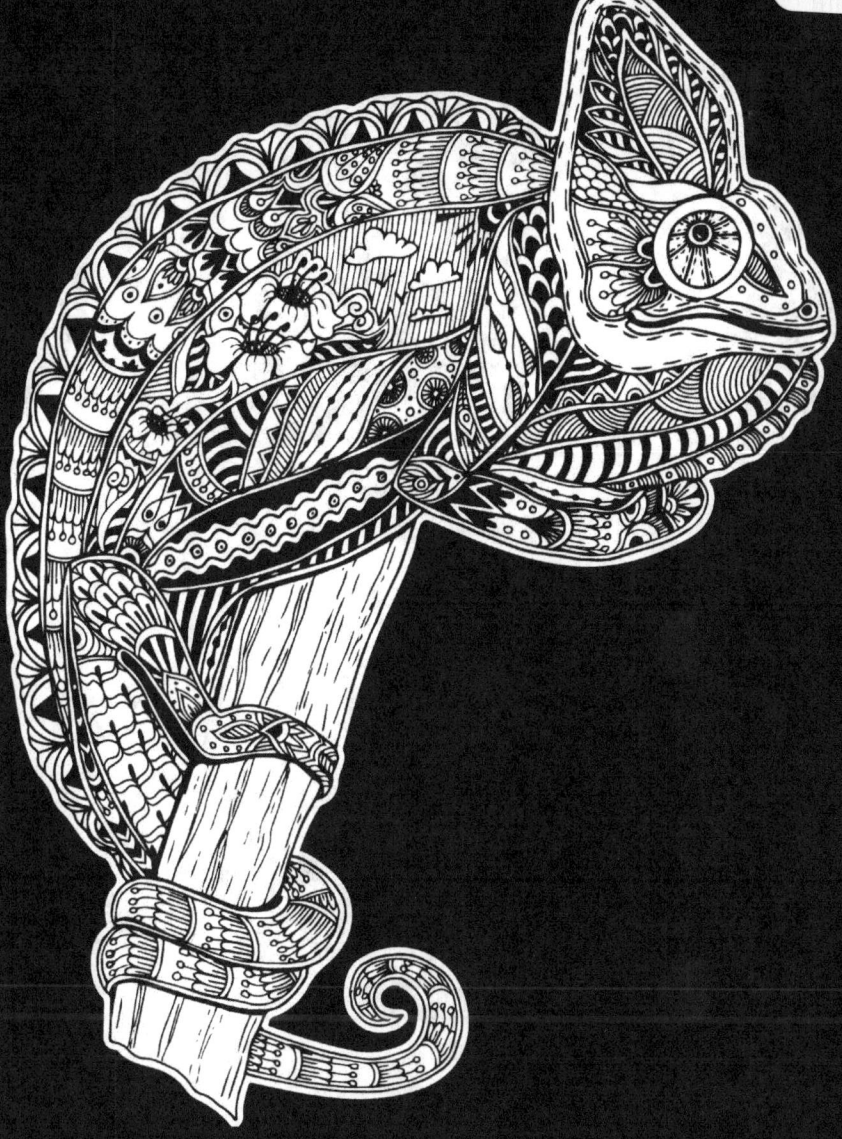

TEEN BOYS
COLORING BOOK
ANIMAL DESIGNS

▲ ART THERAPY
COLORING

Preview of Coloring Pages

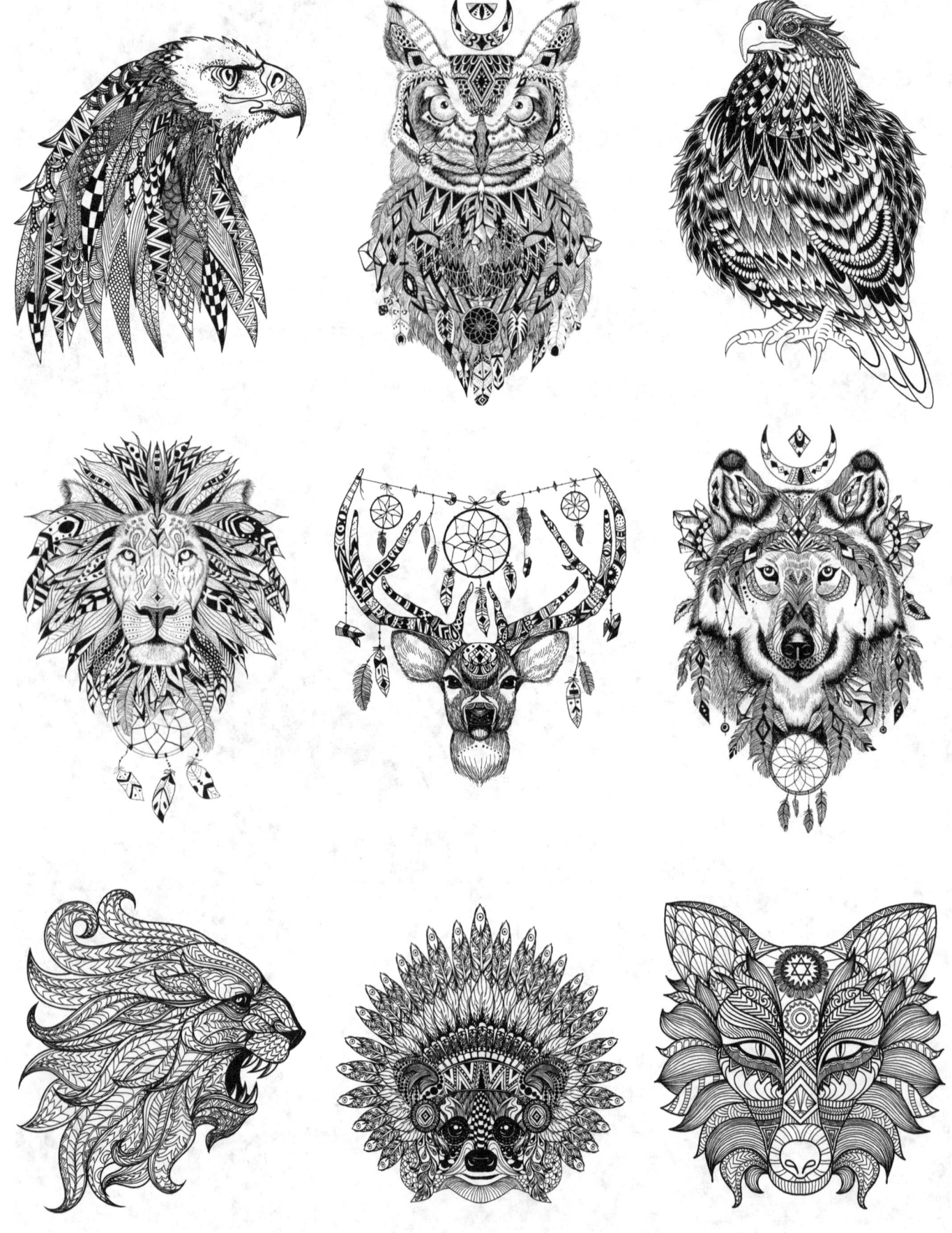

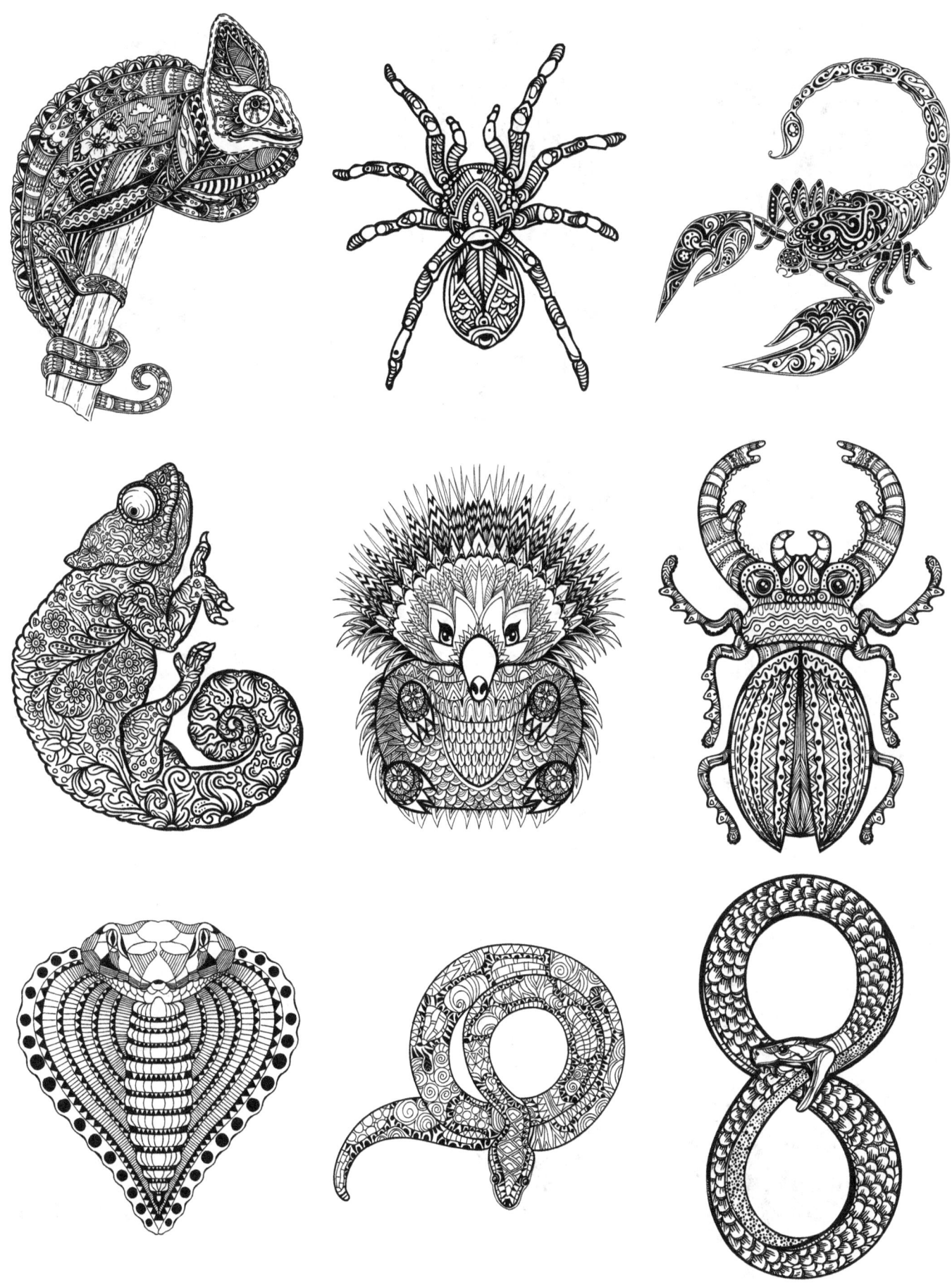

Preview of Coloring Pages

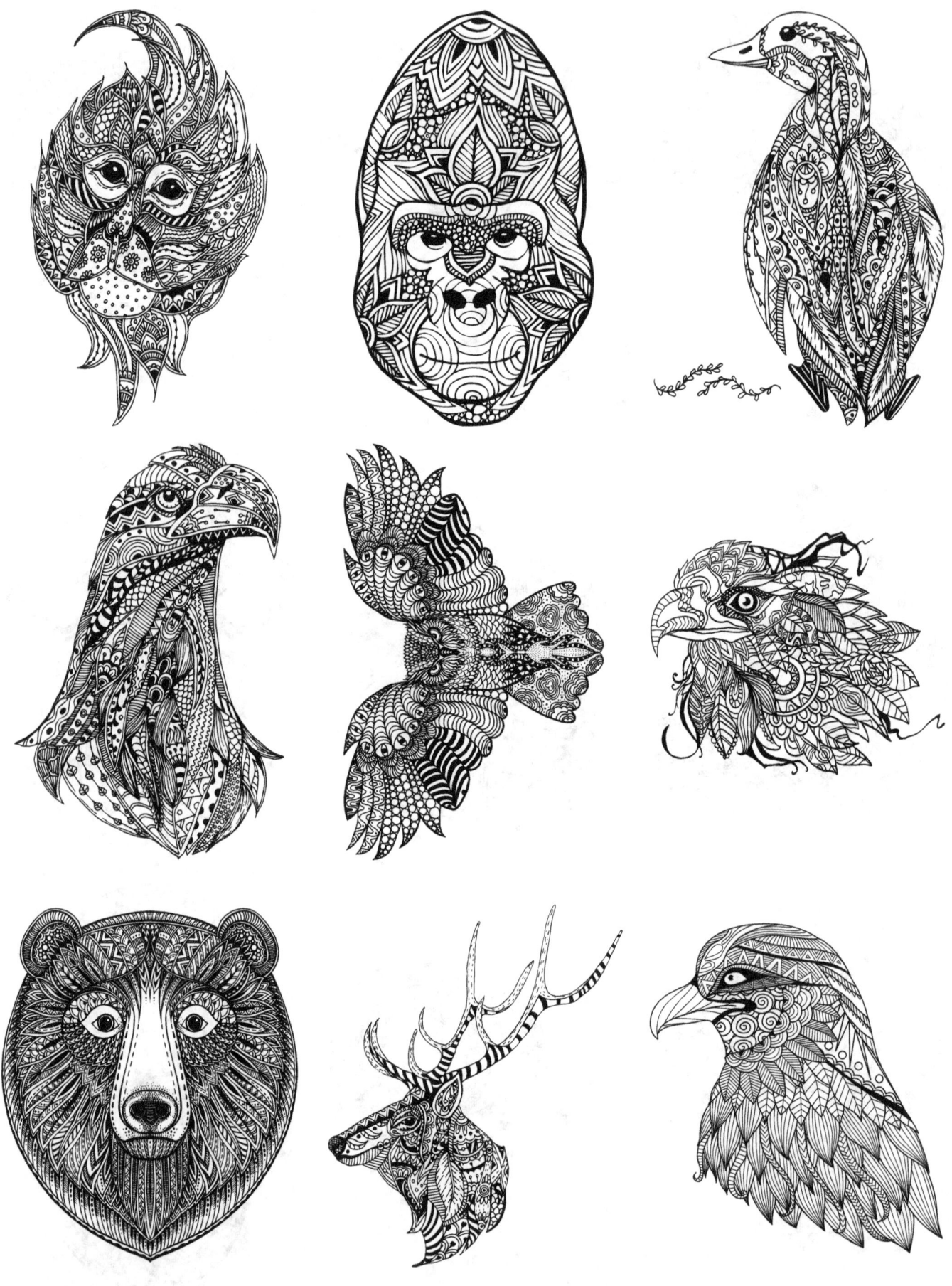

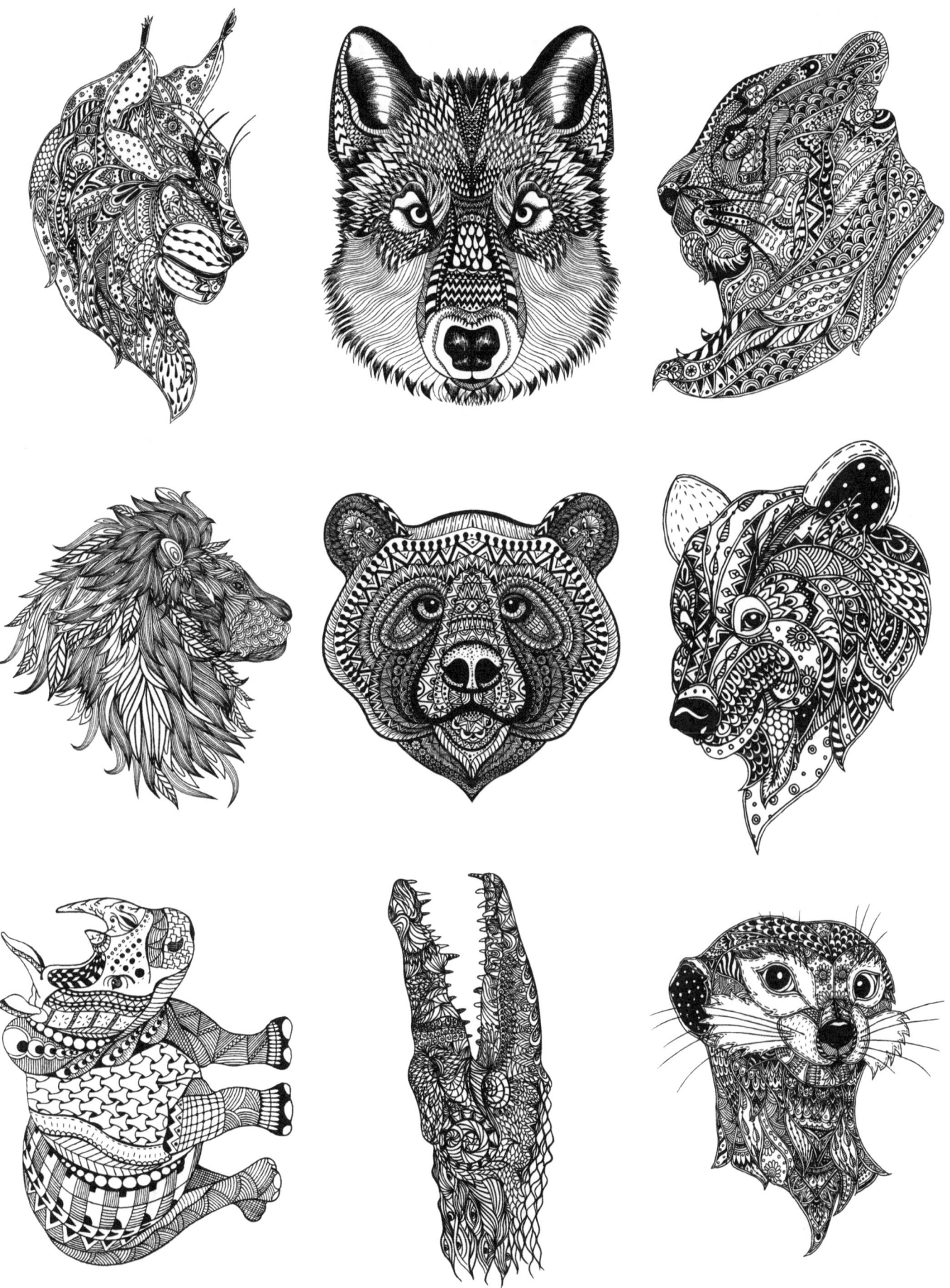

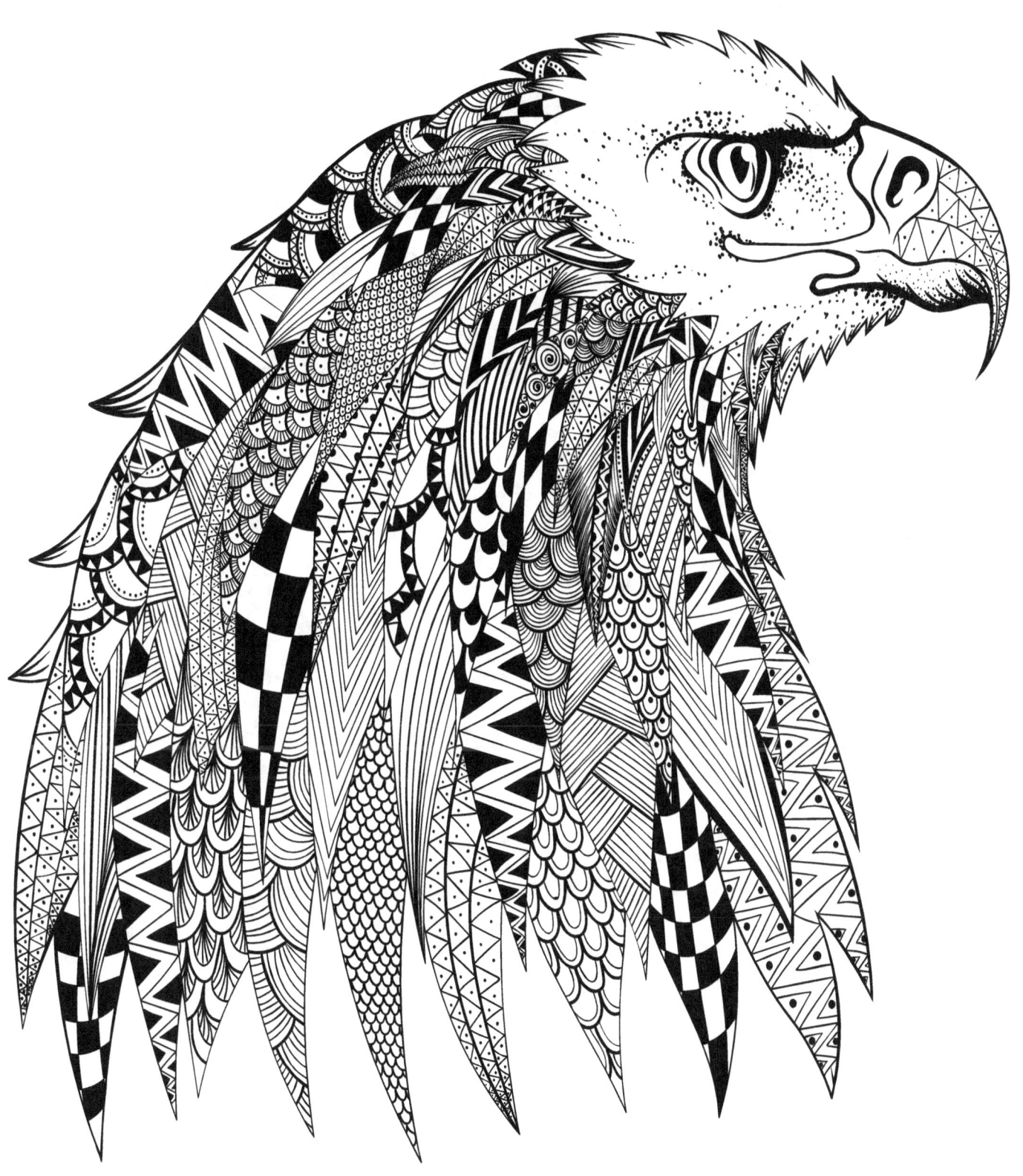

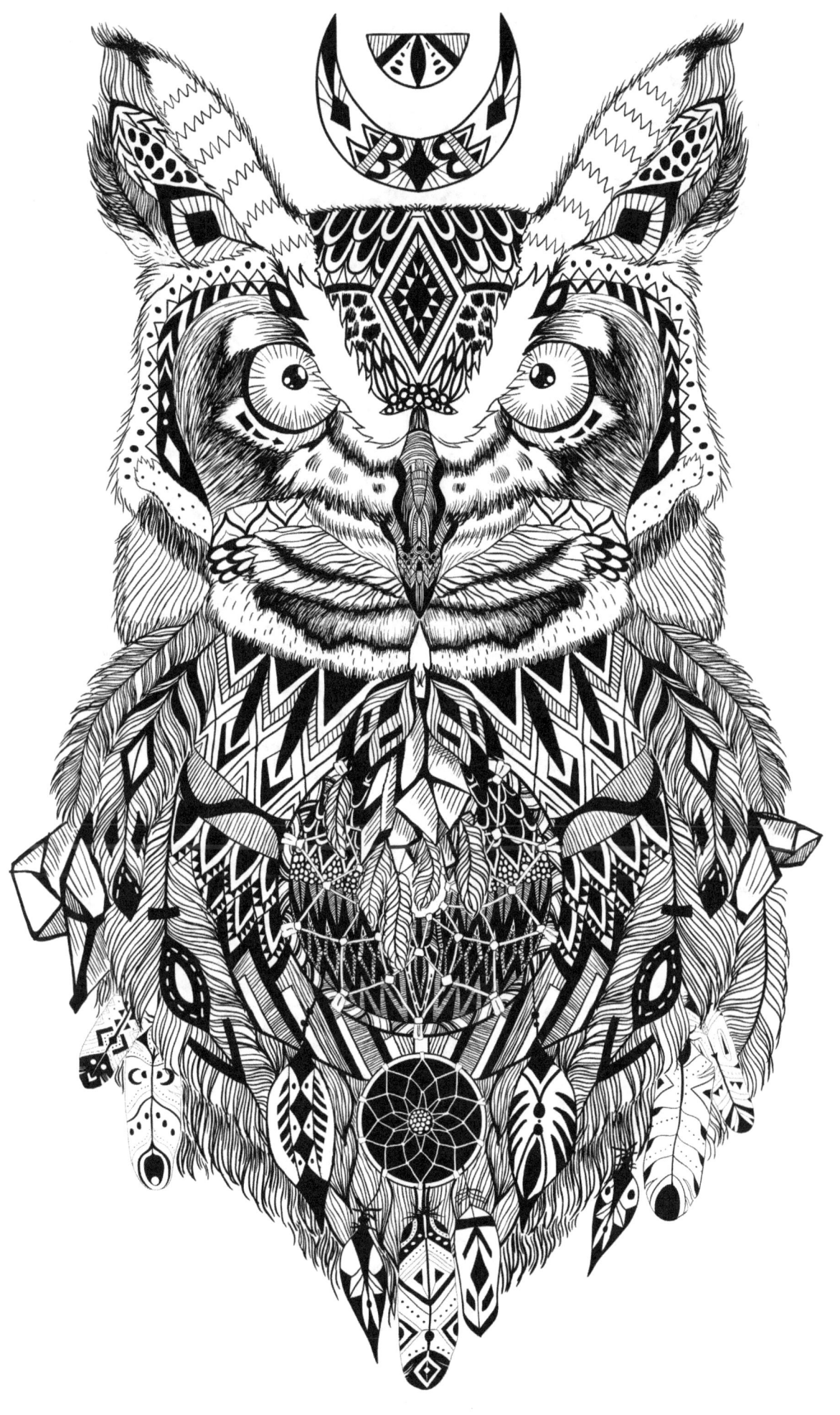

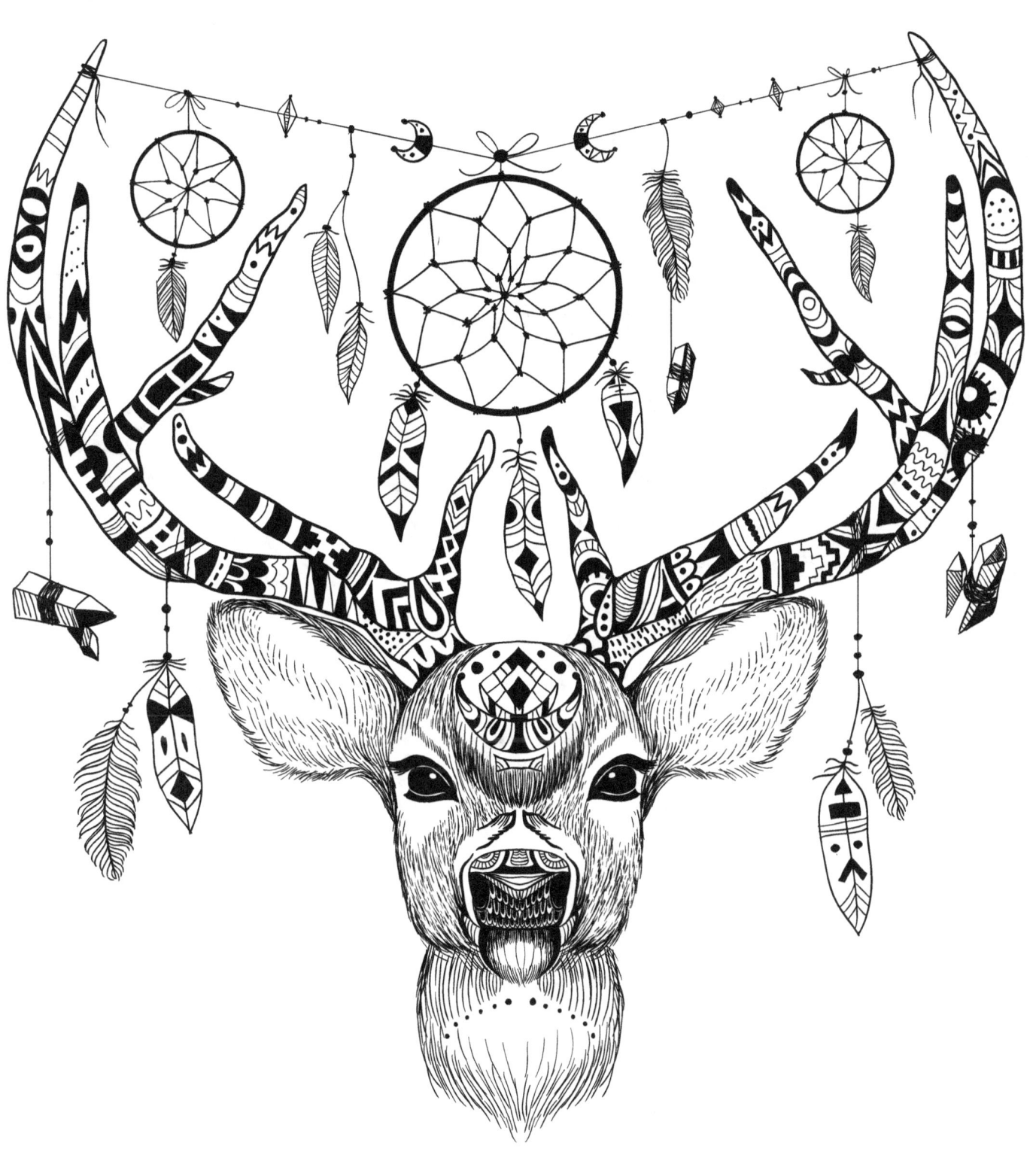

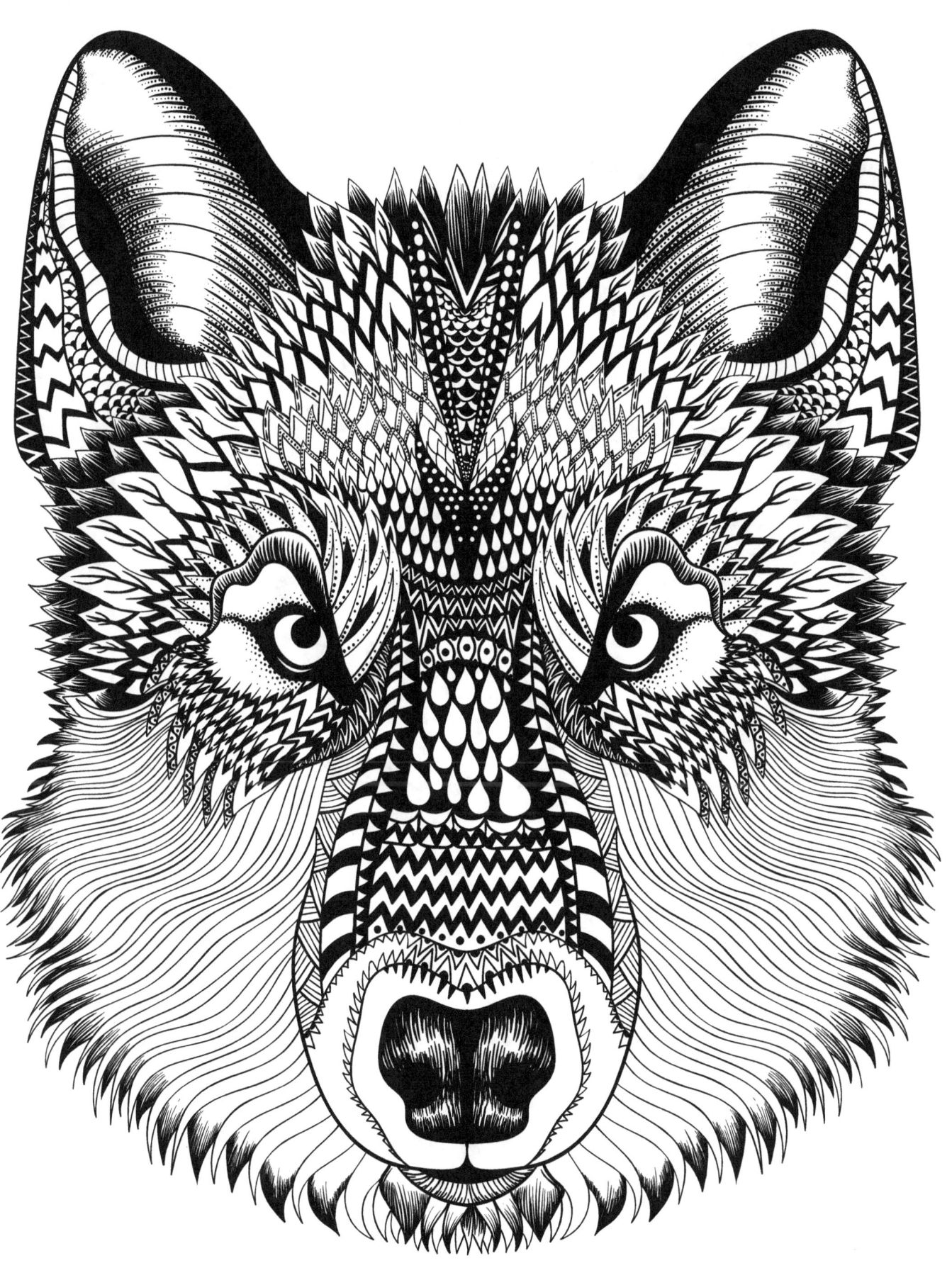

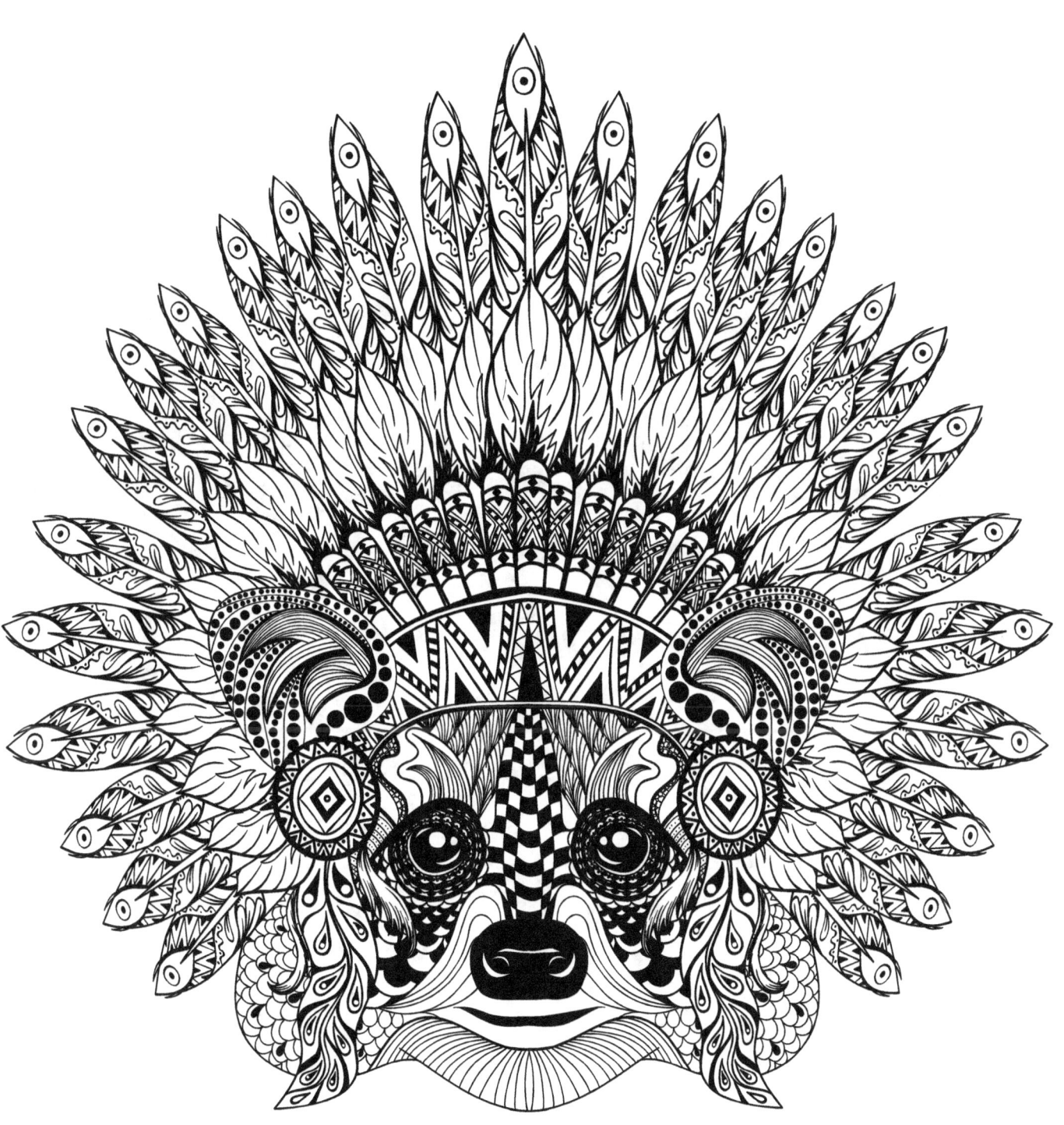

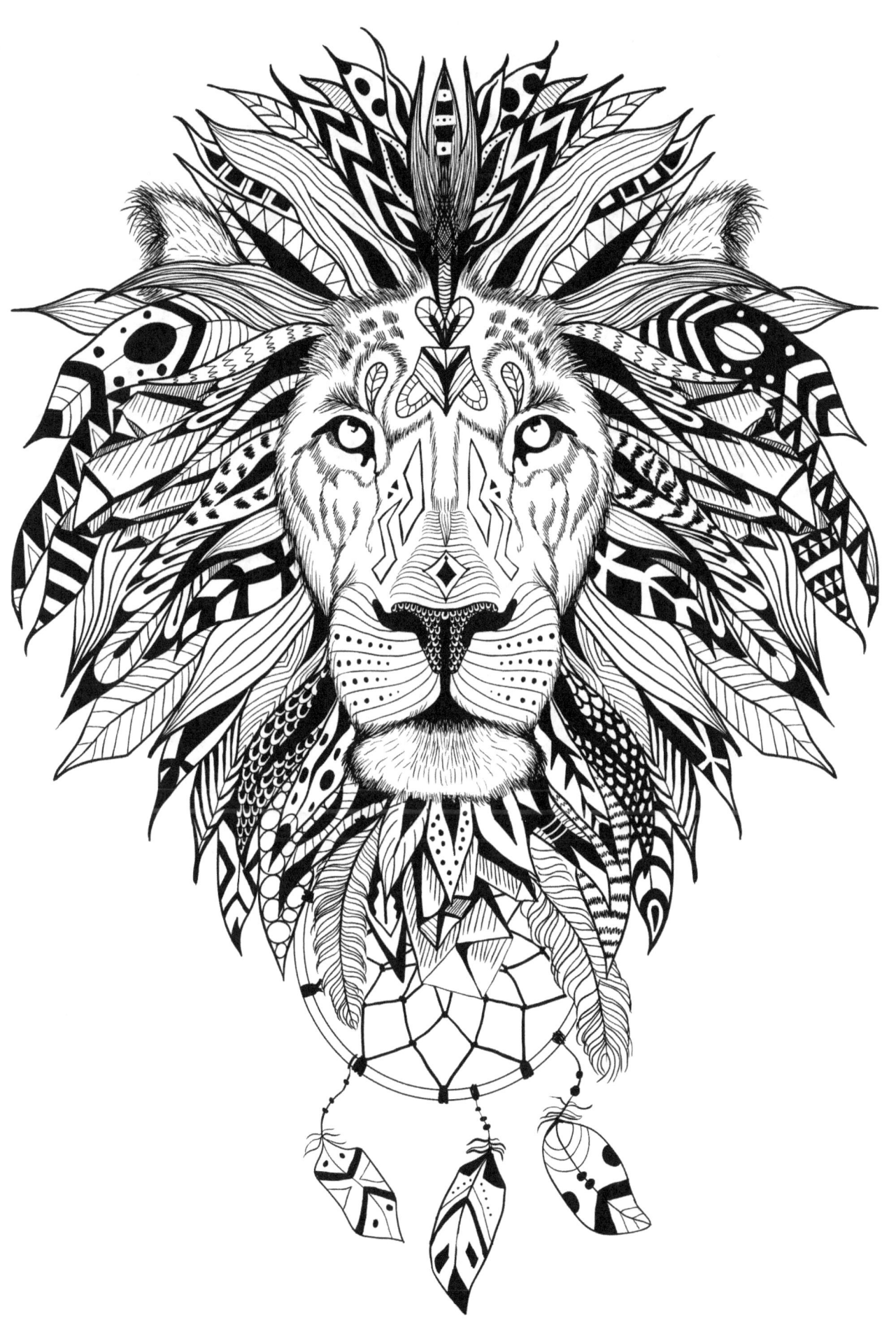

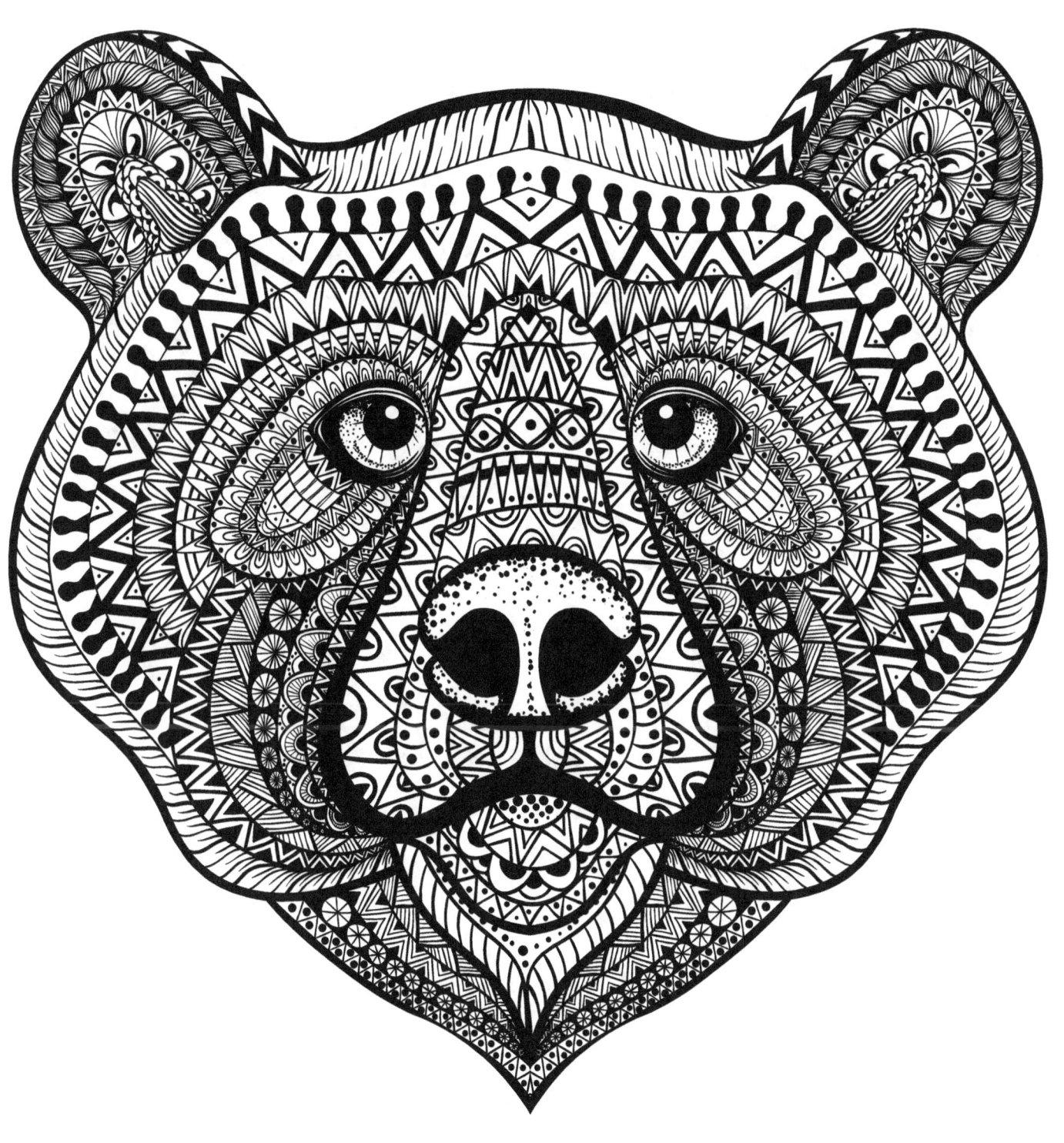

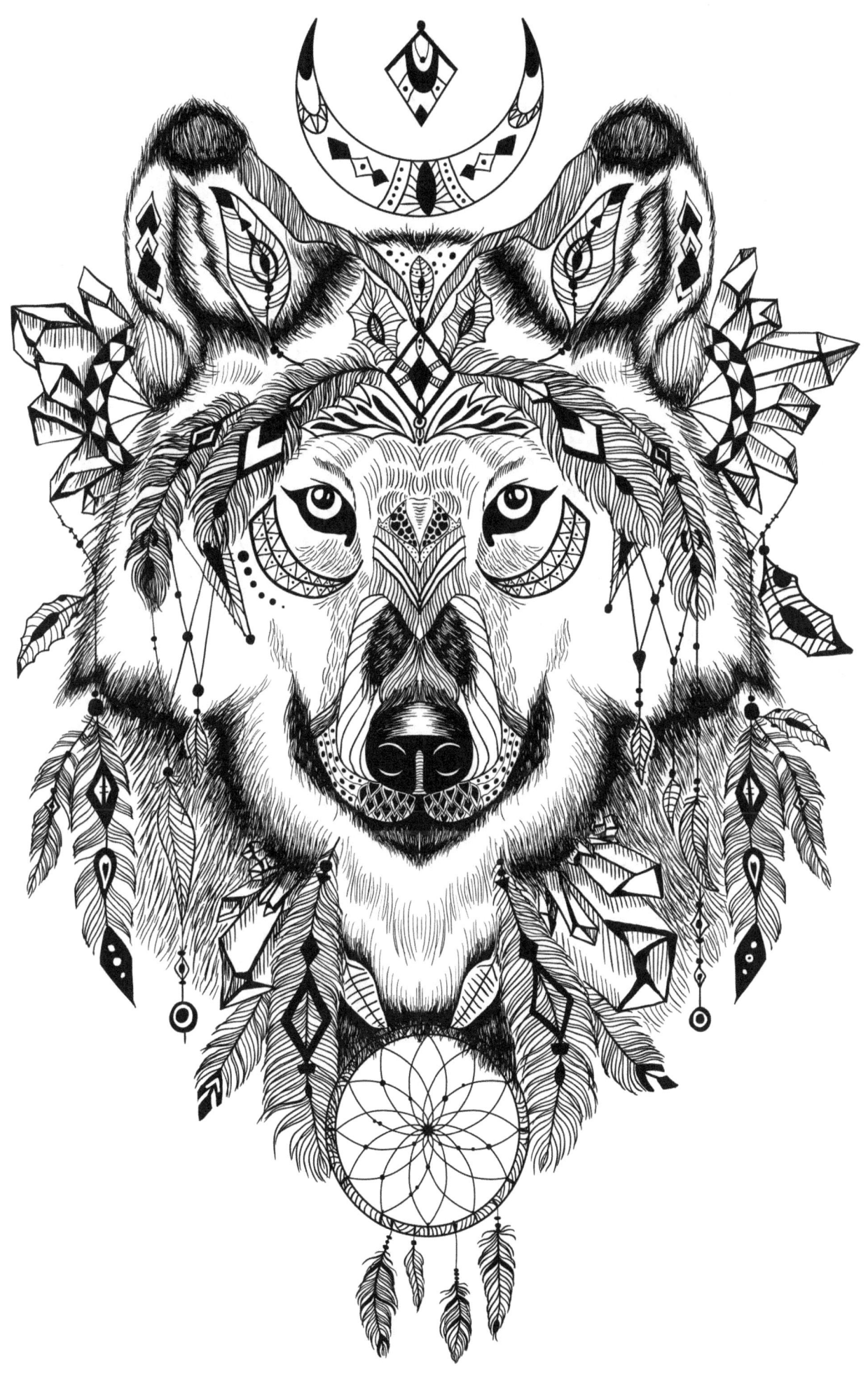

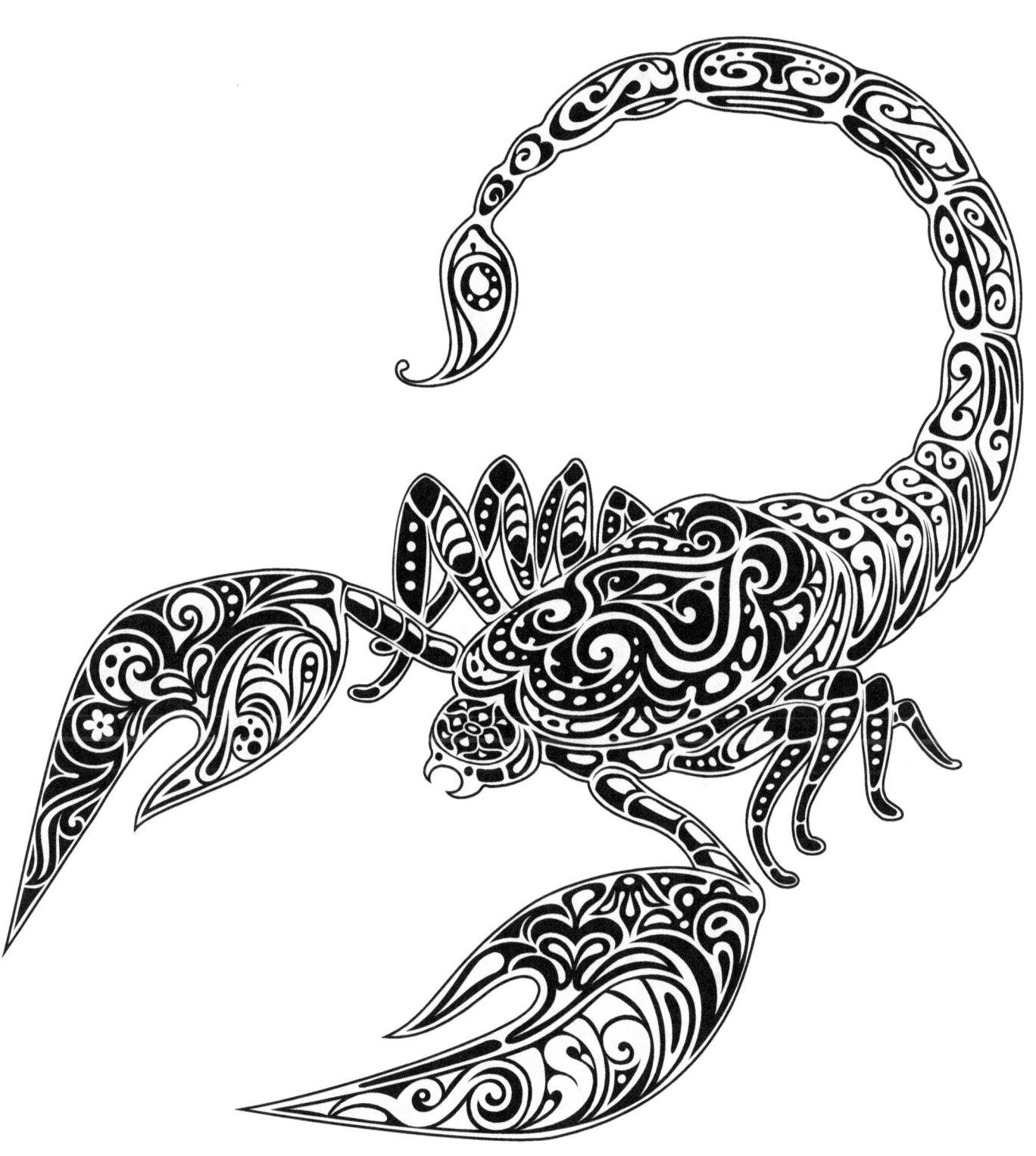

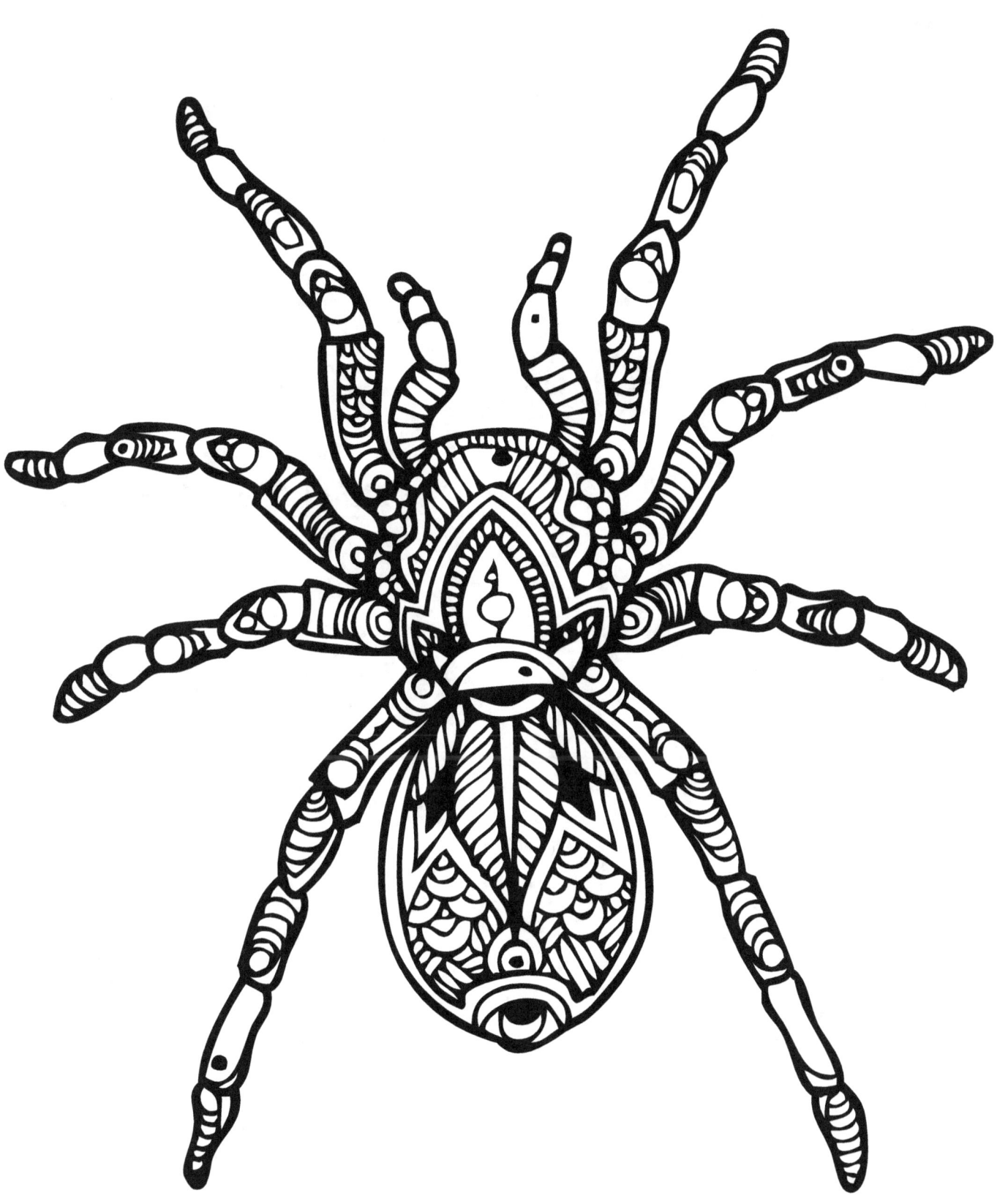

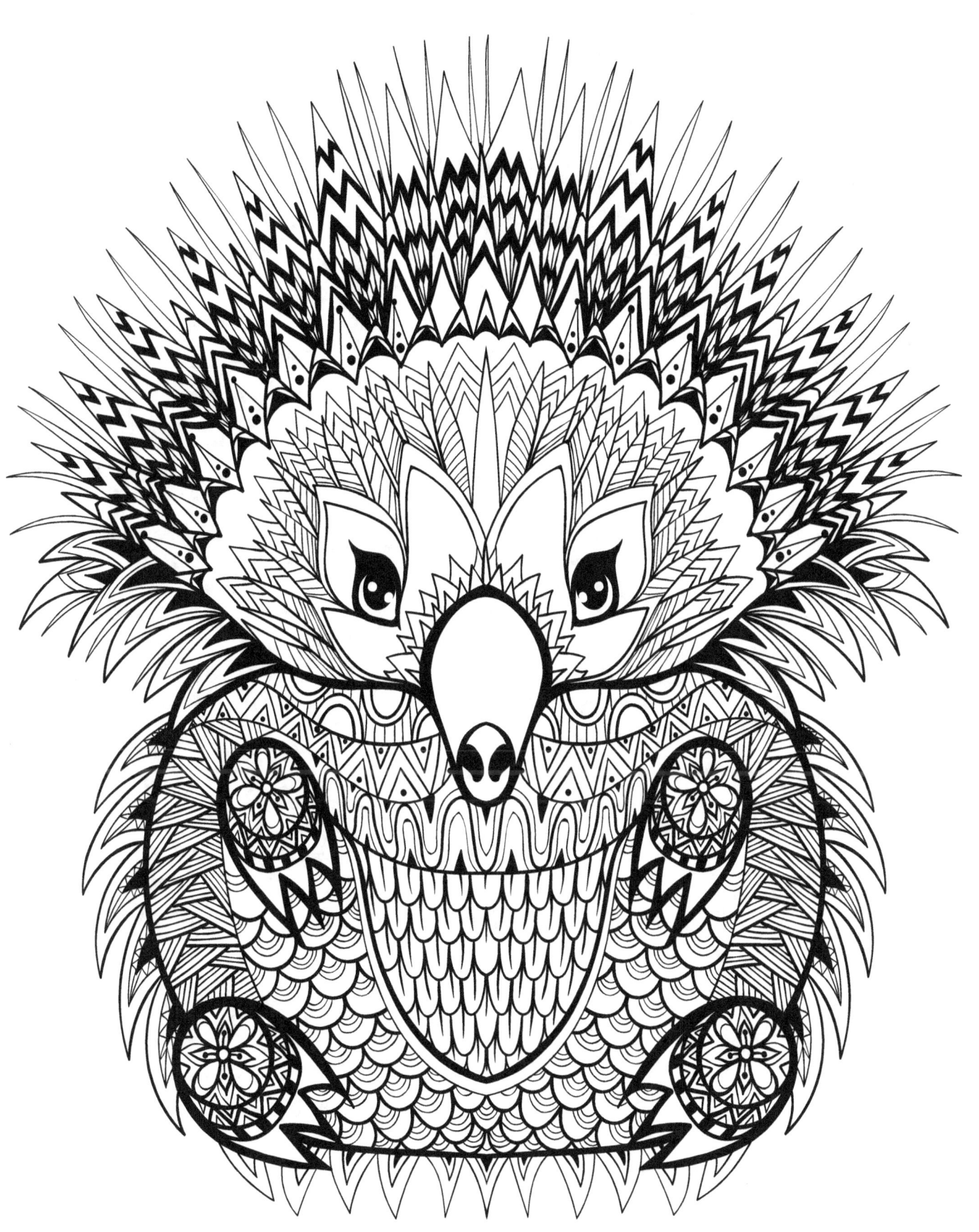

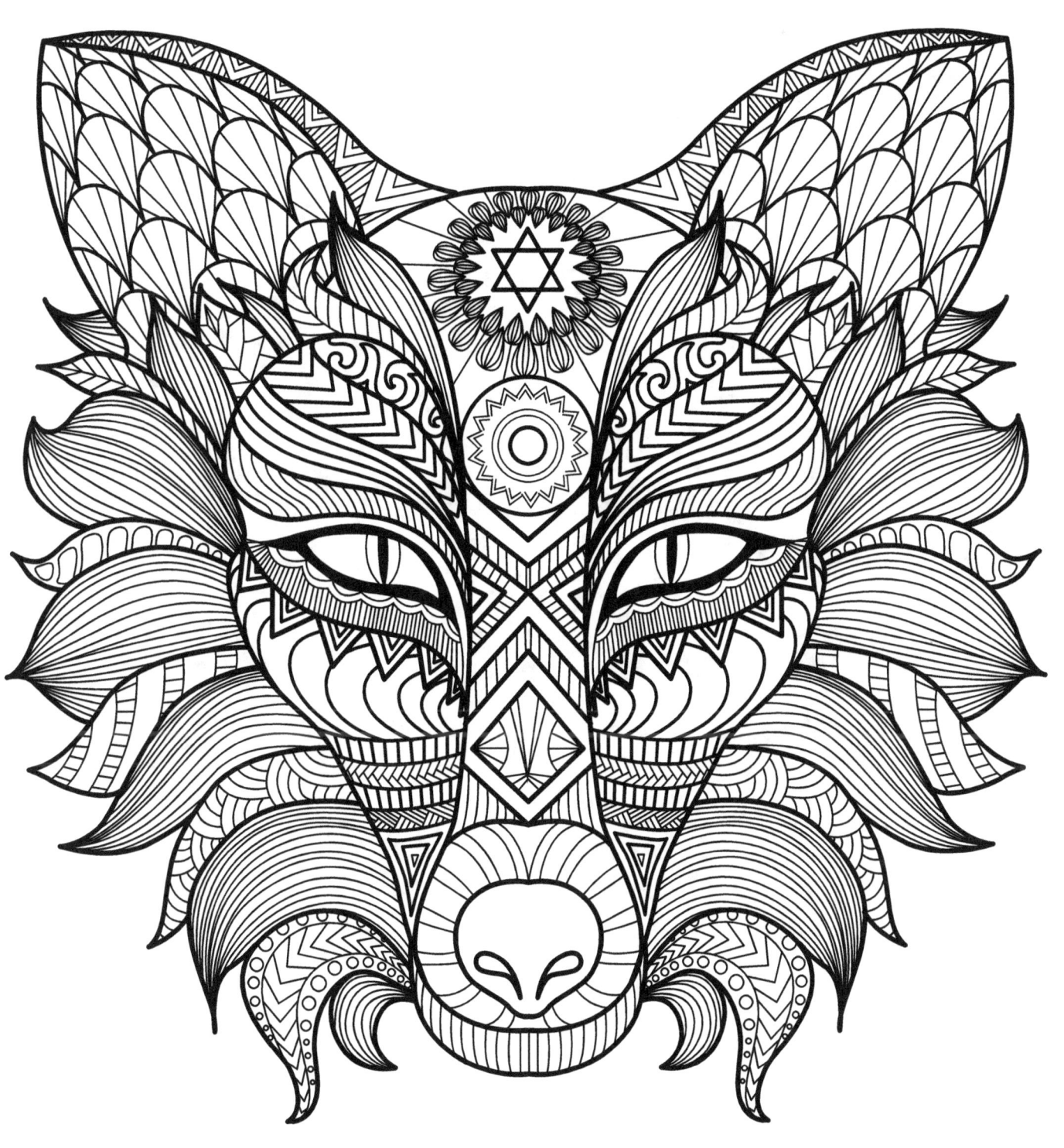

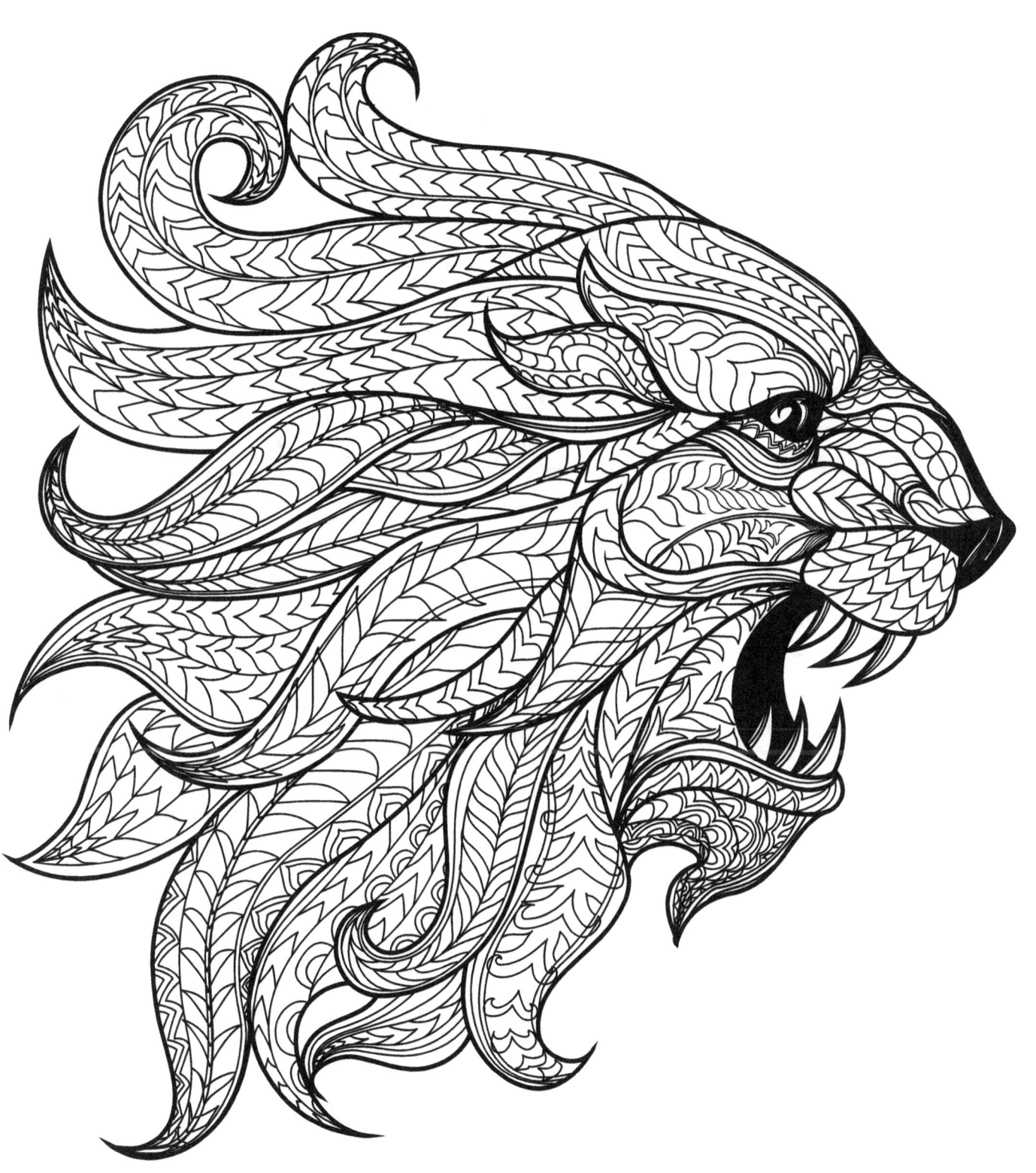

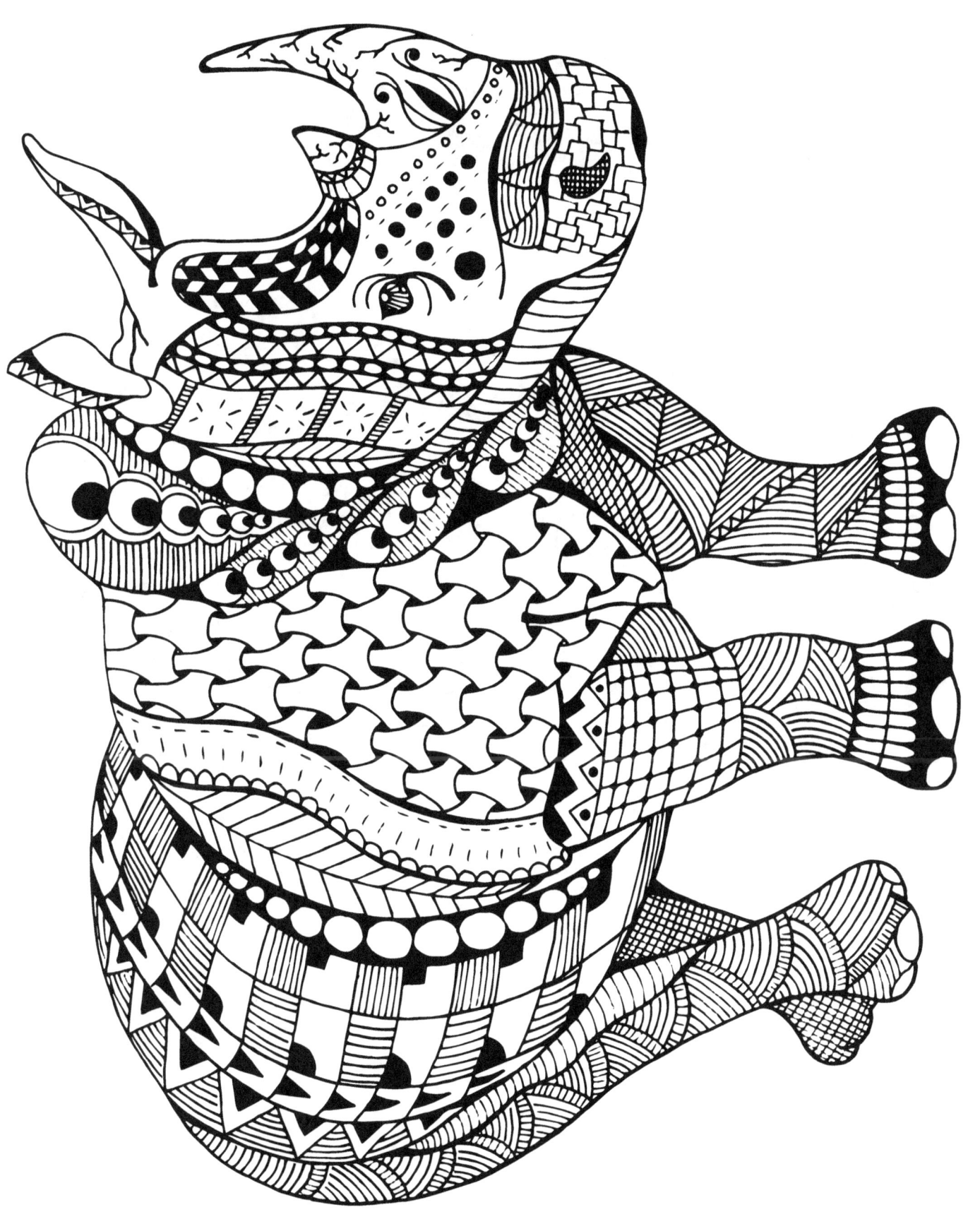

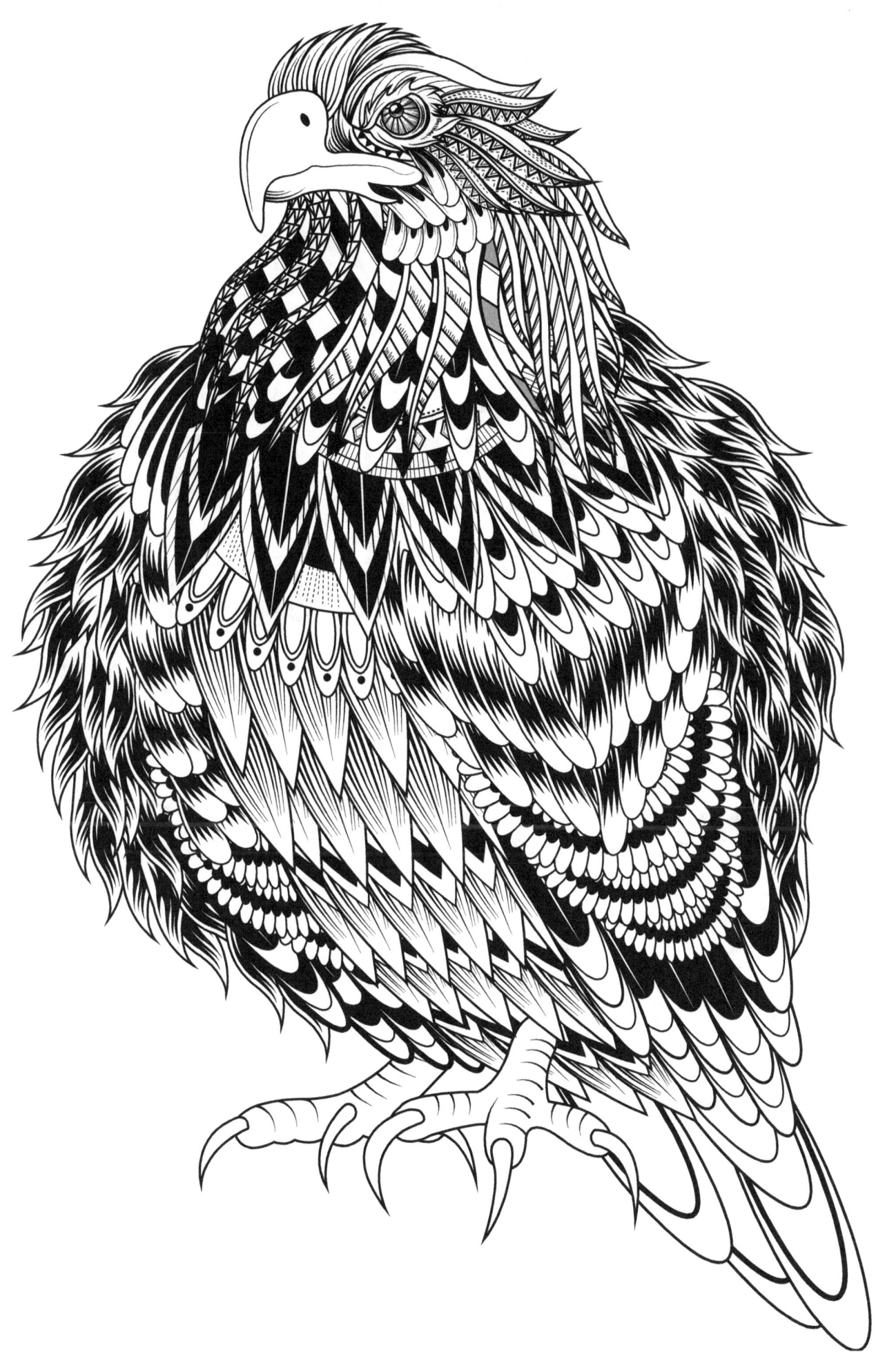

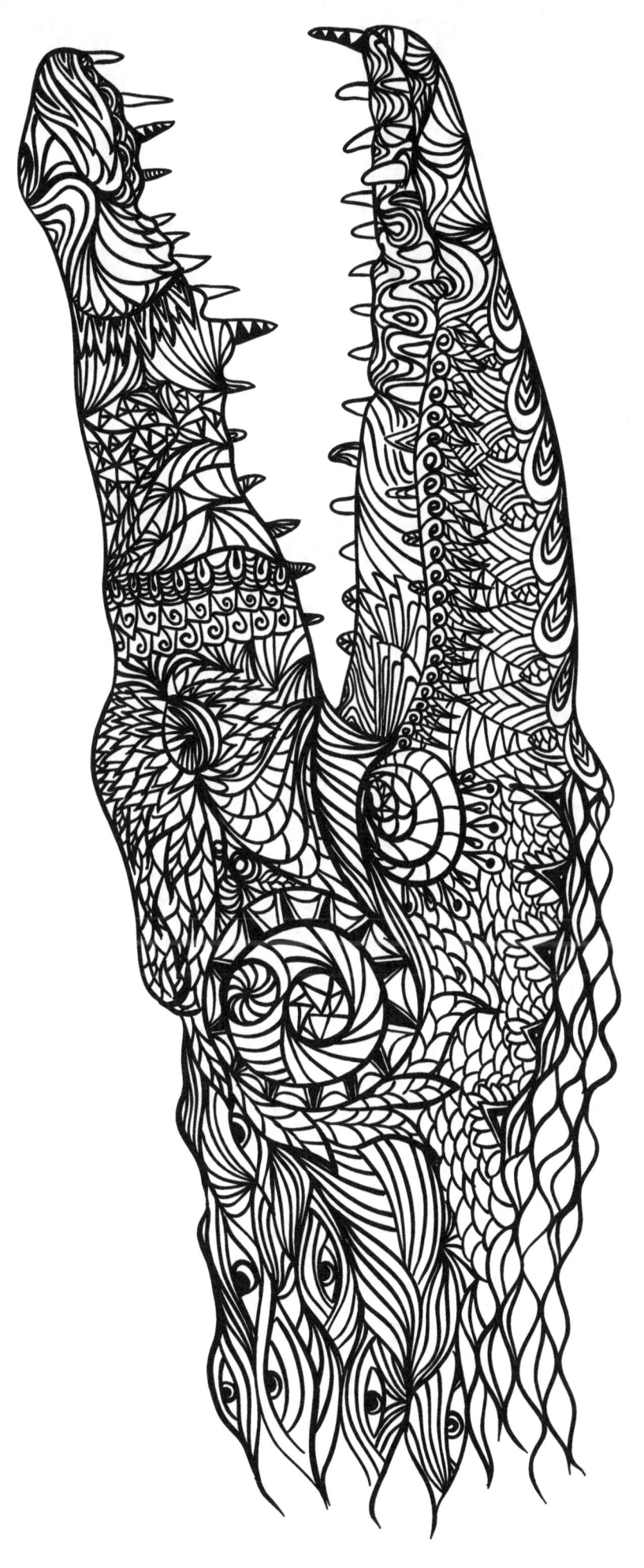

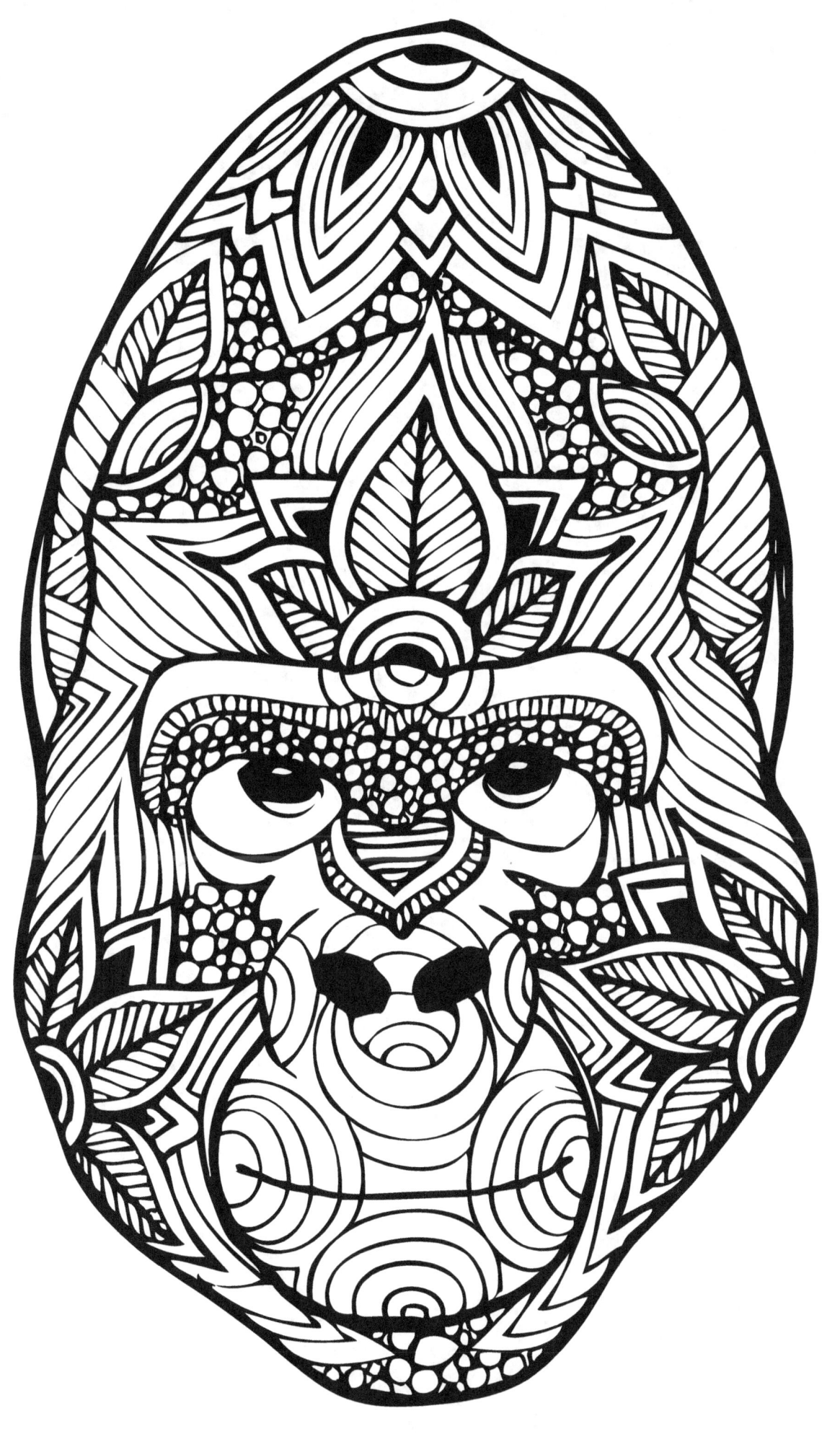

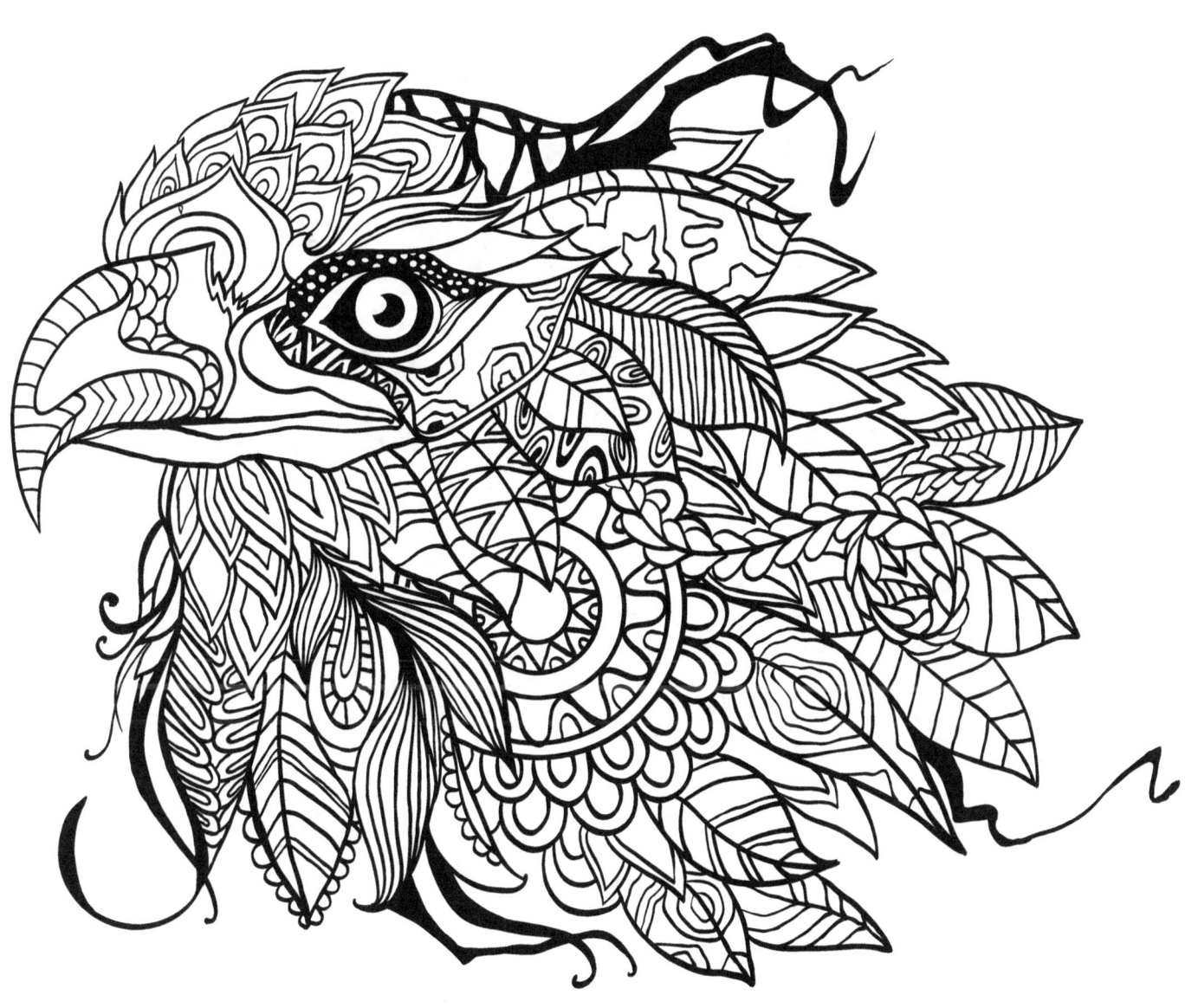

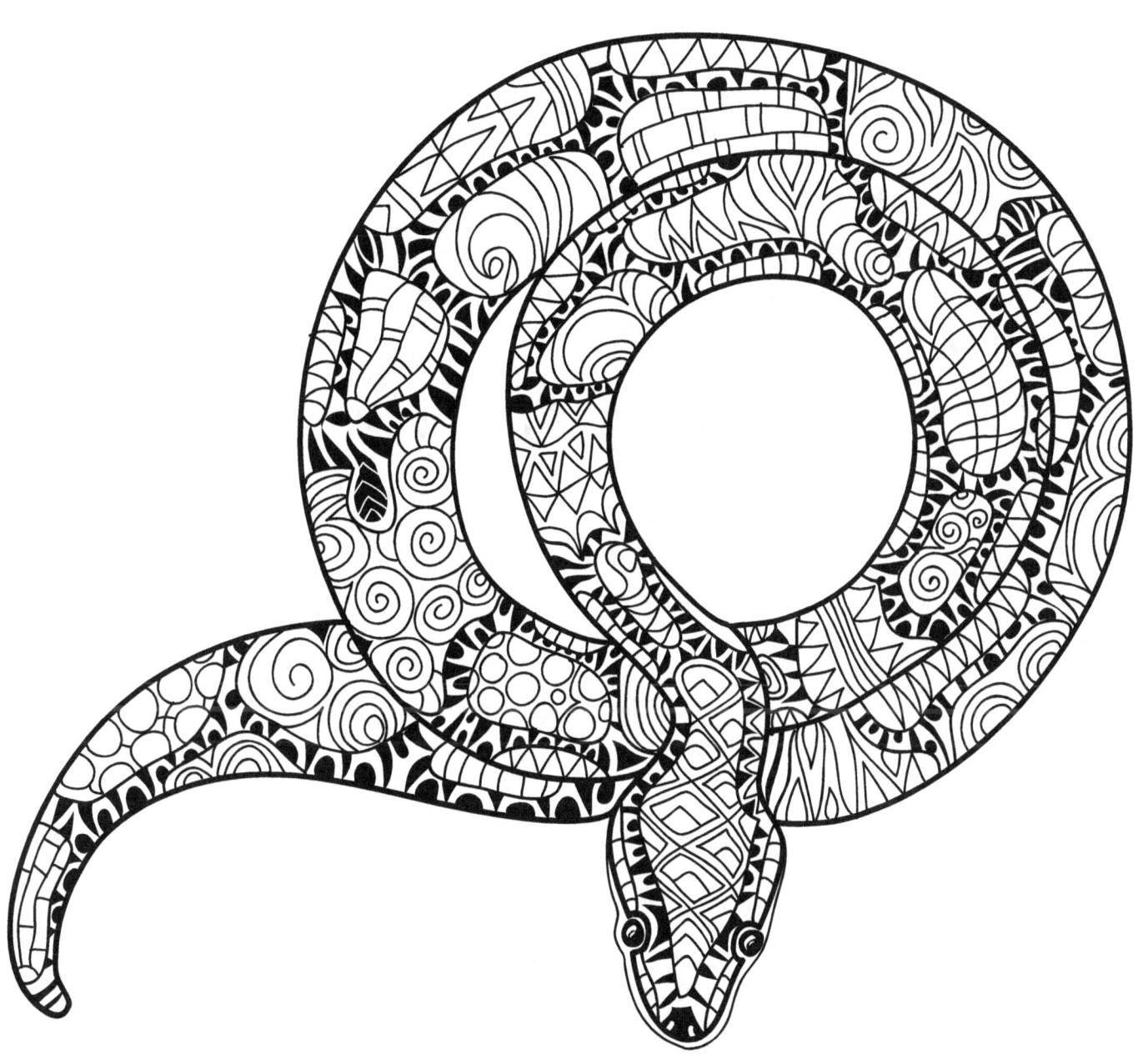

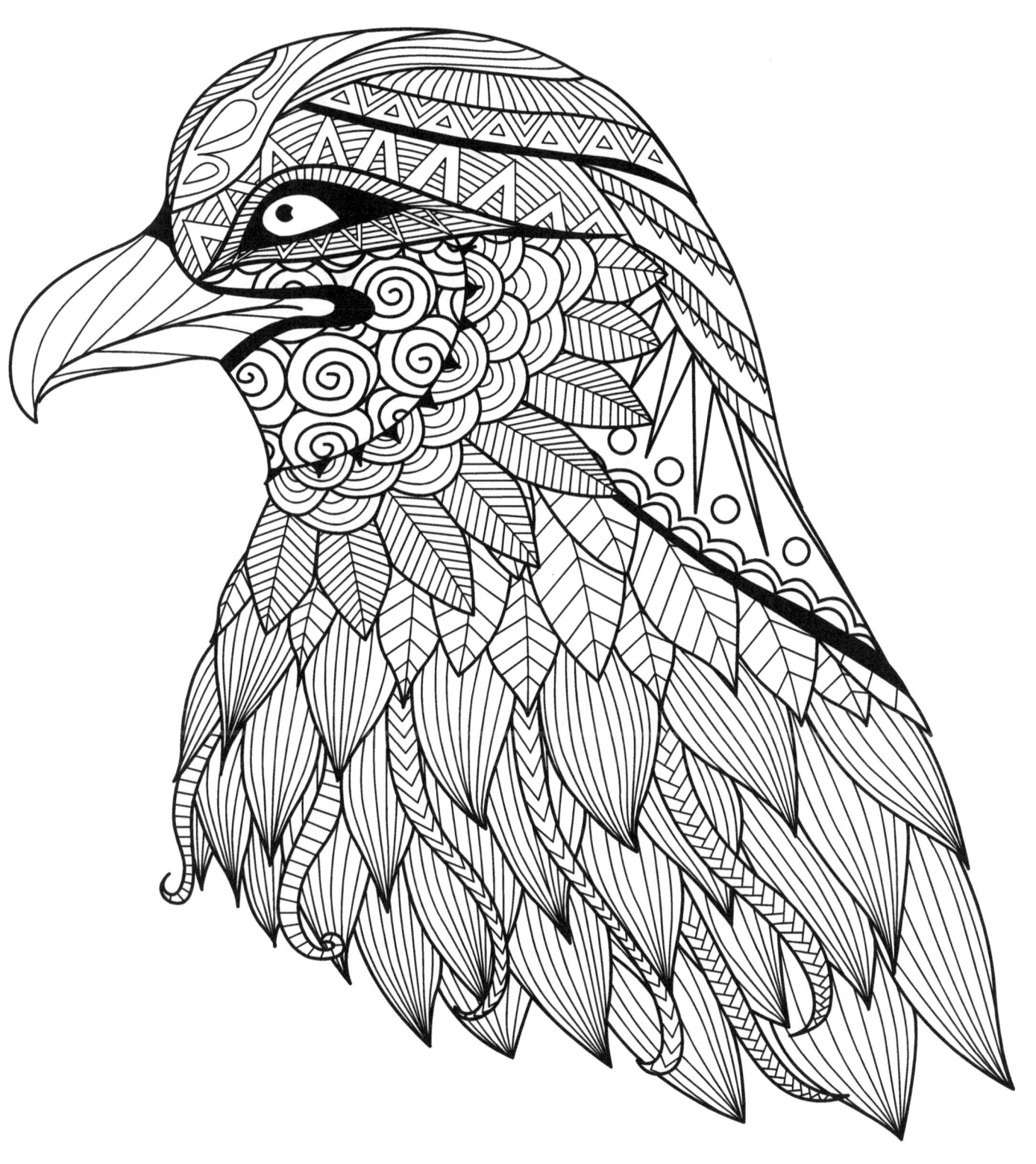

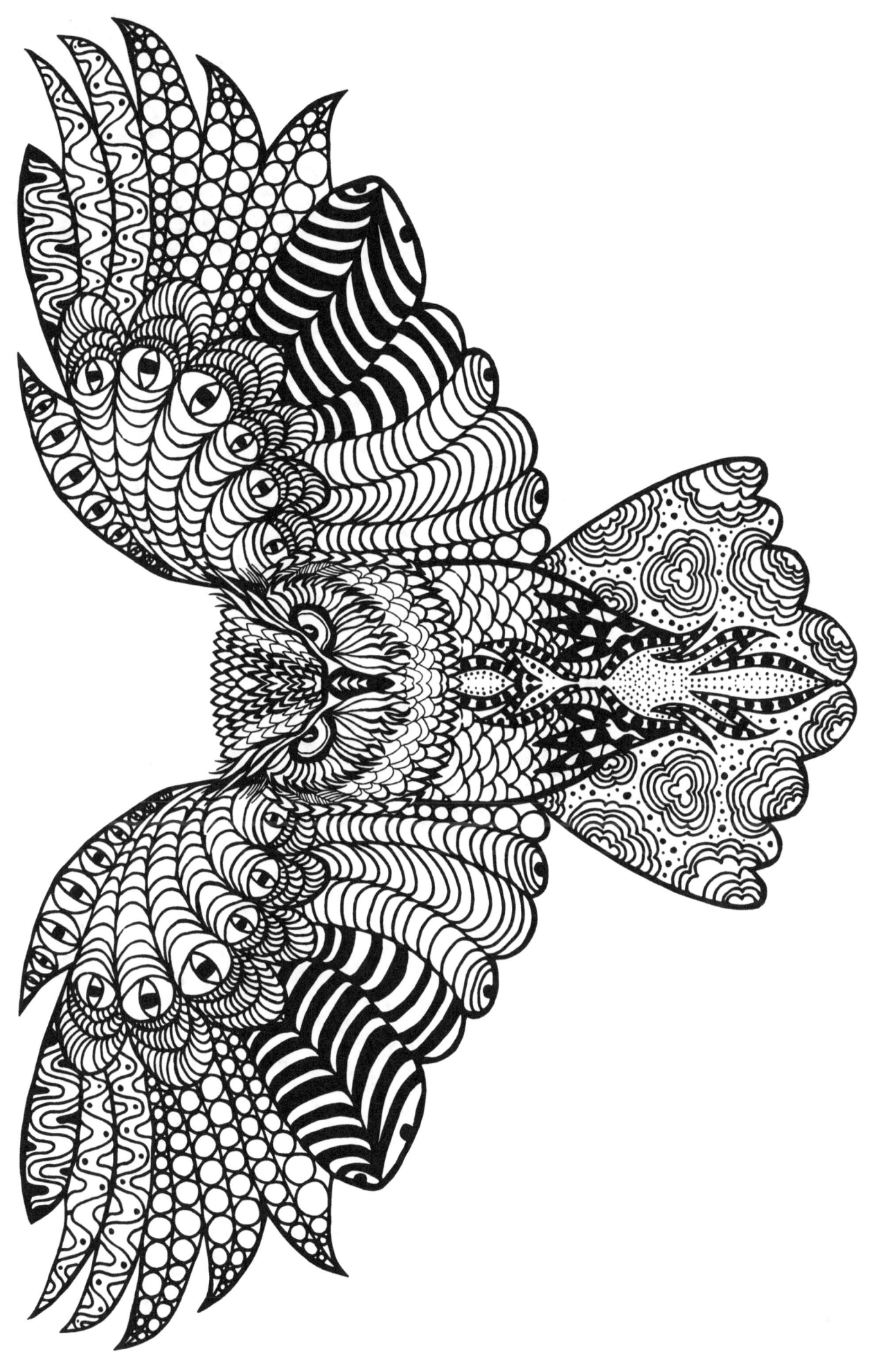

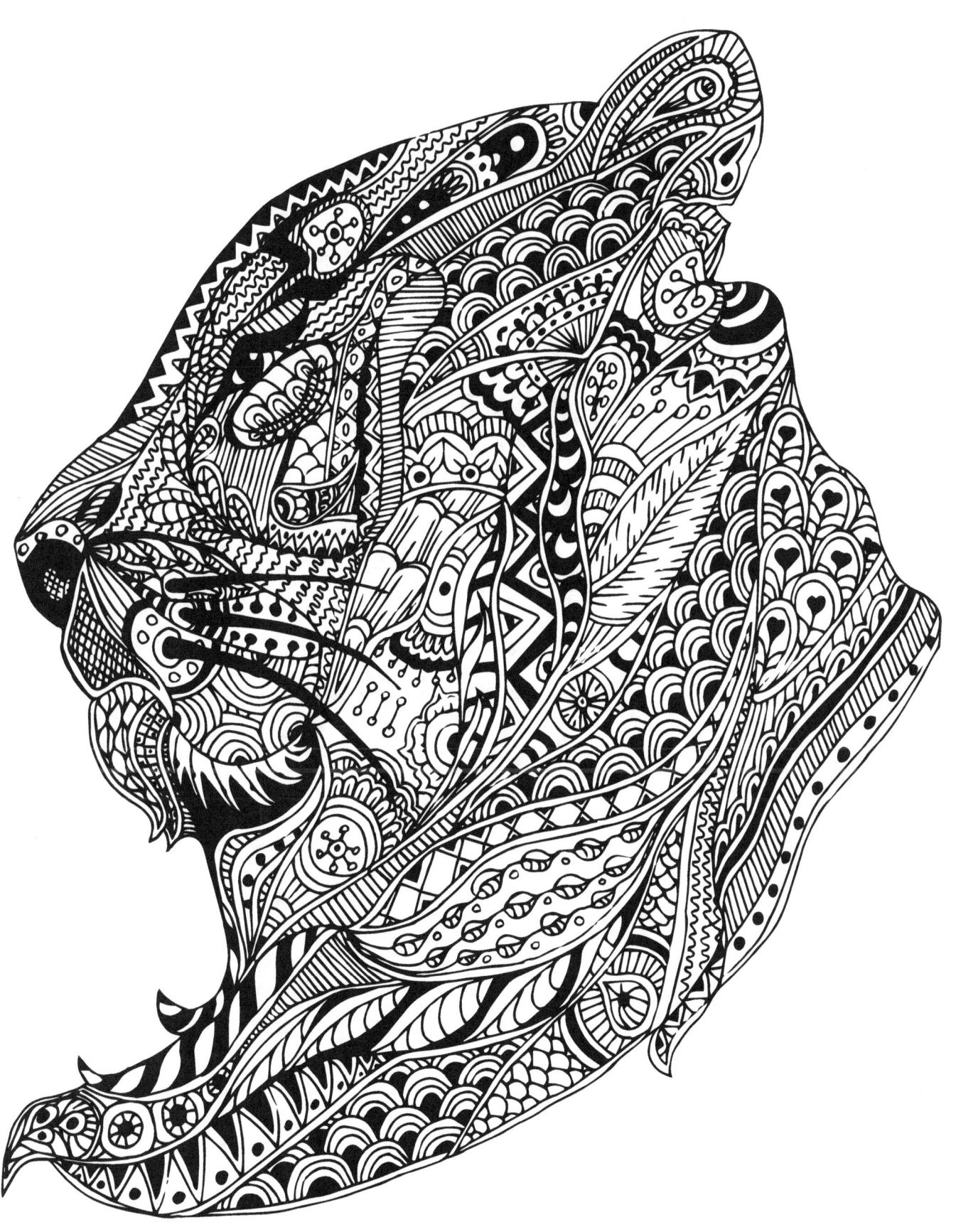

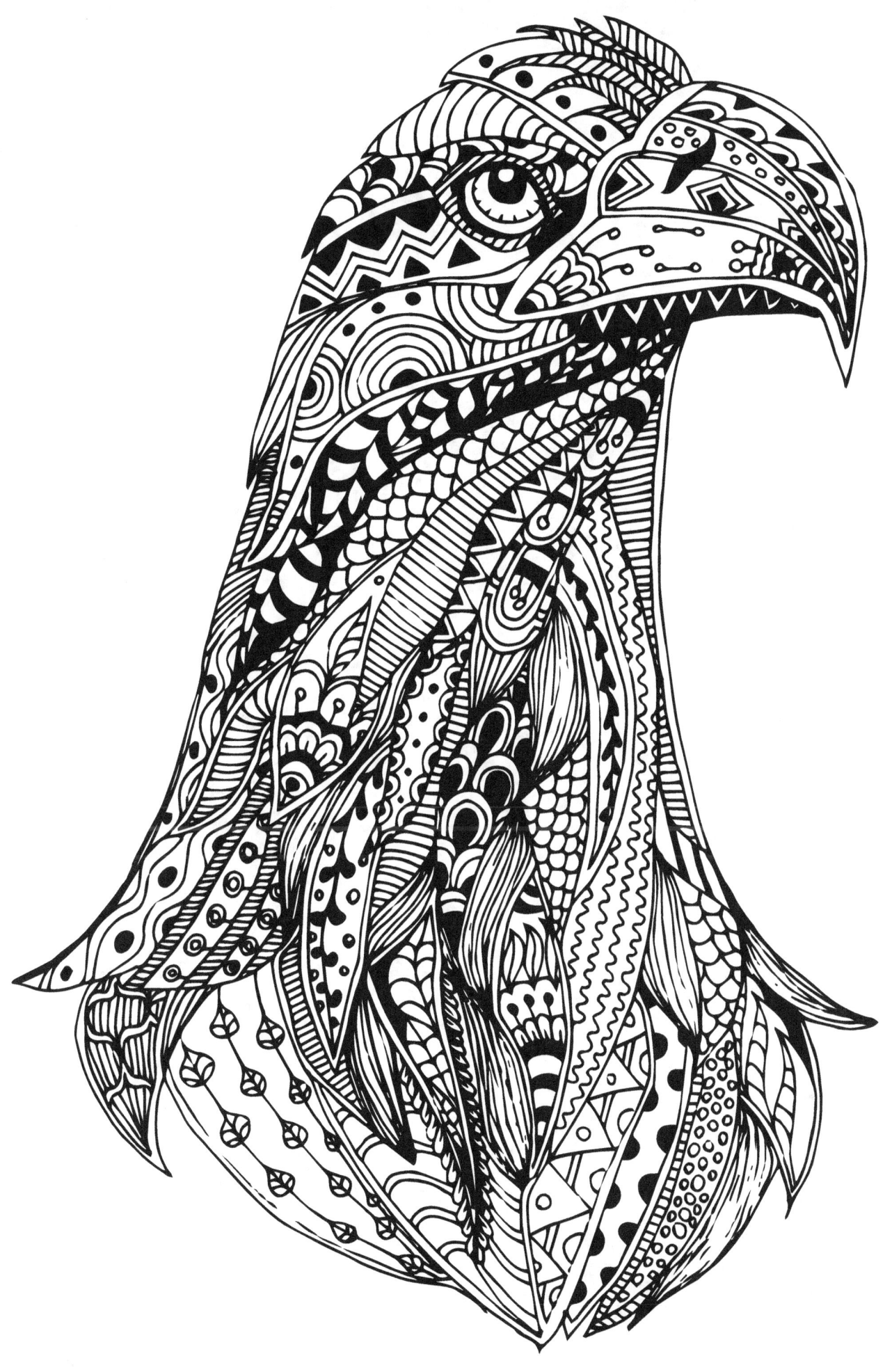

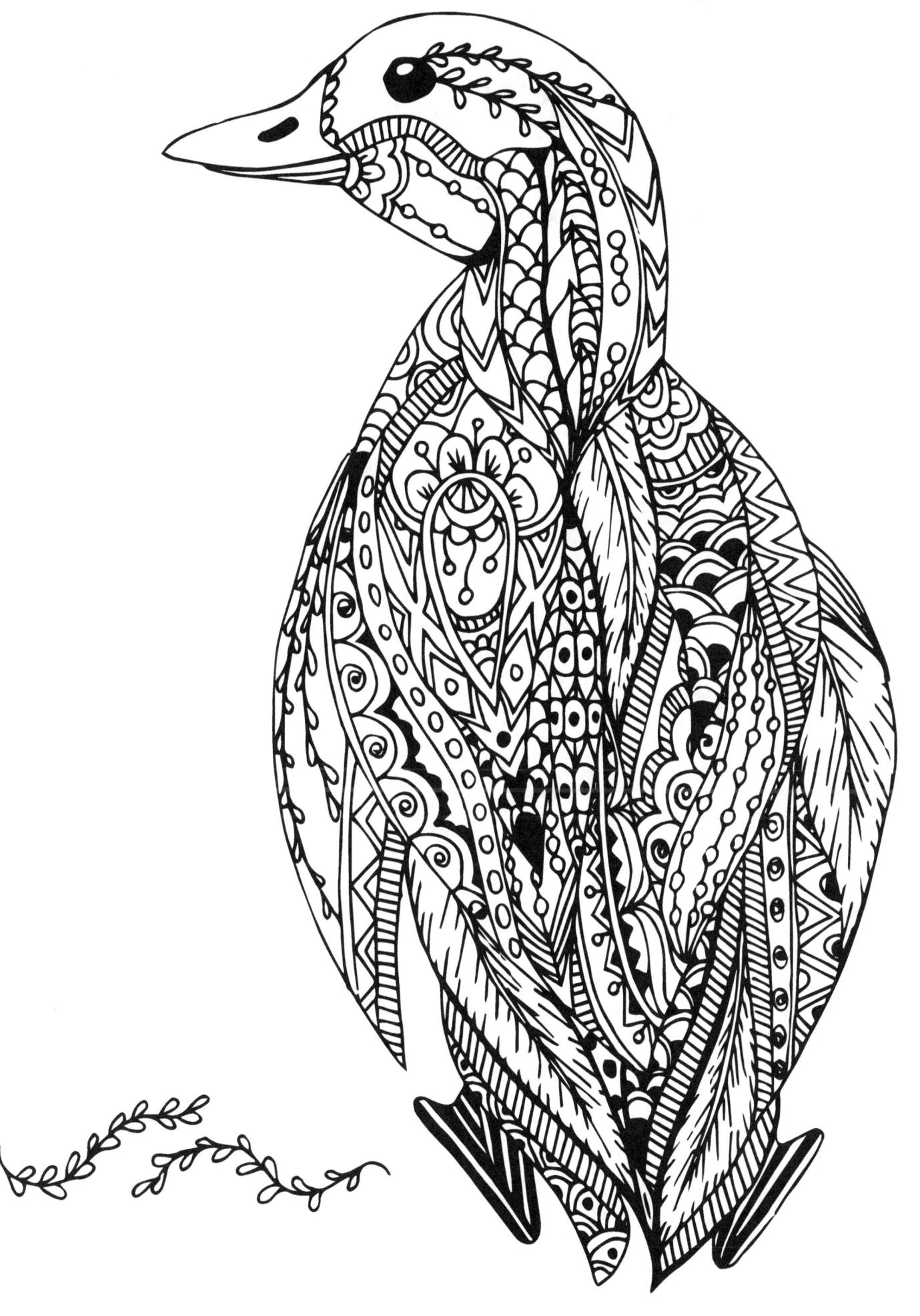

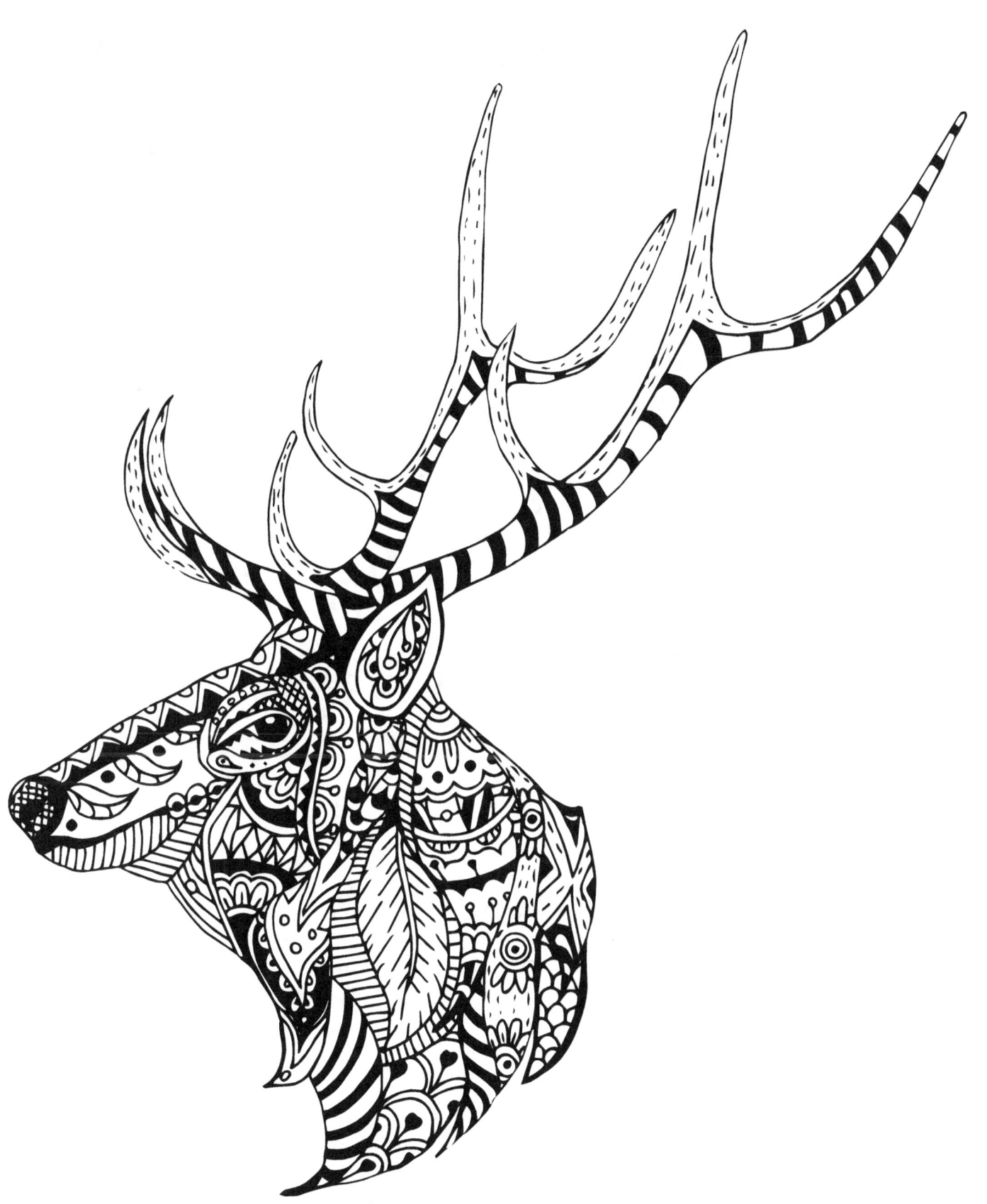

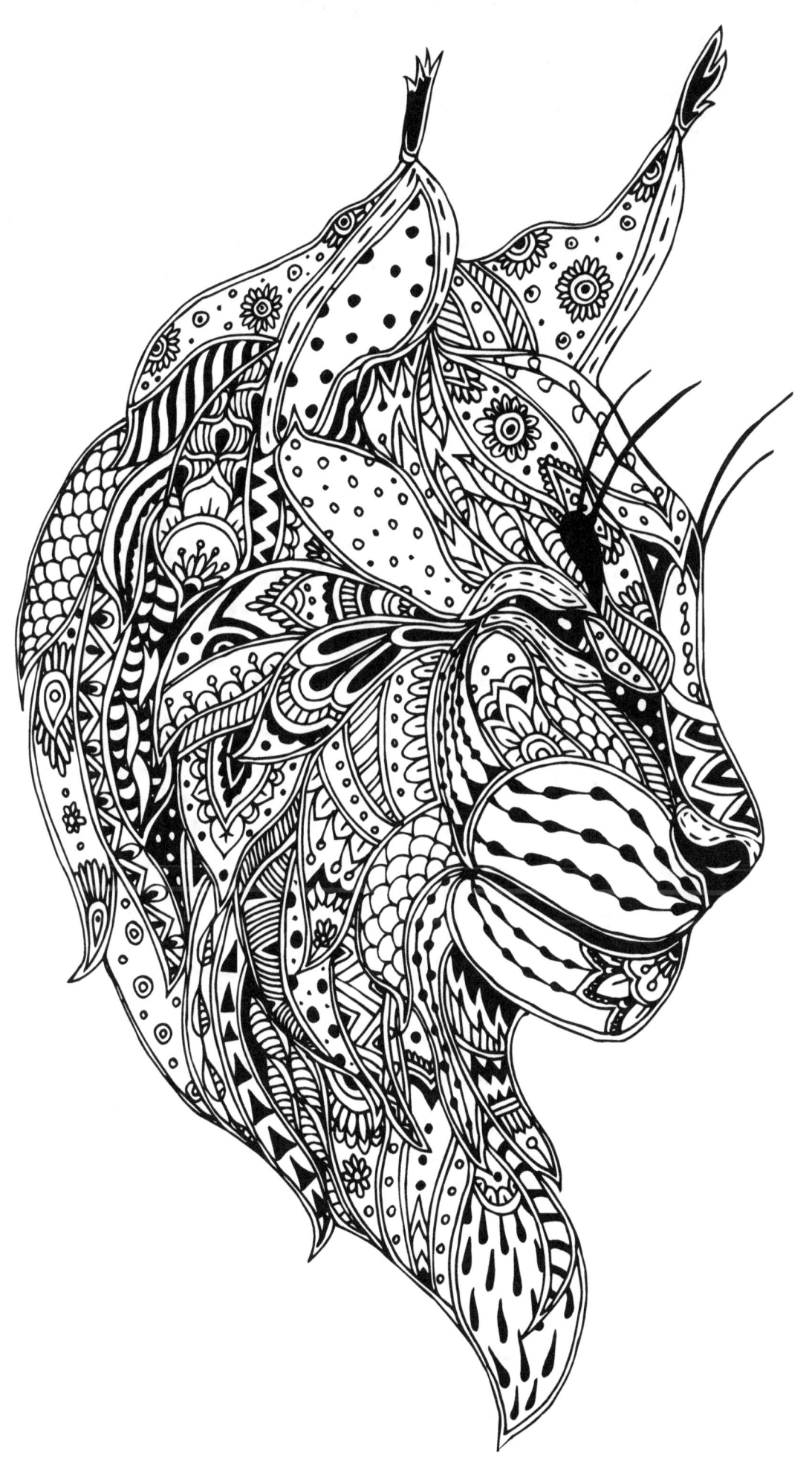

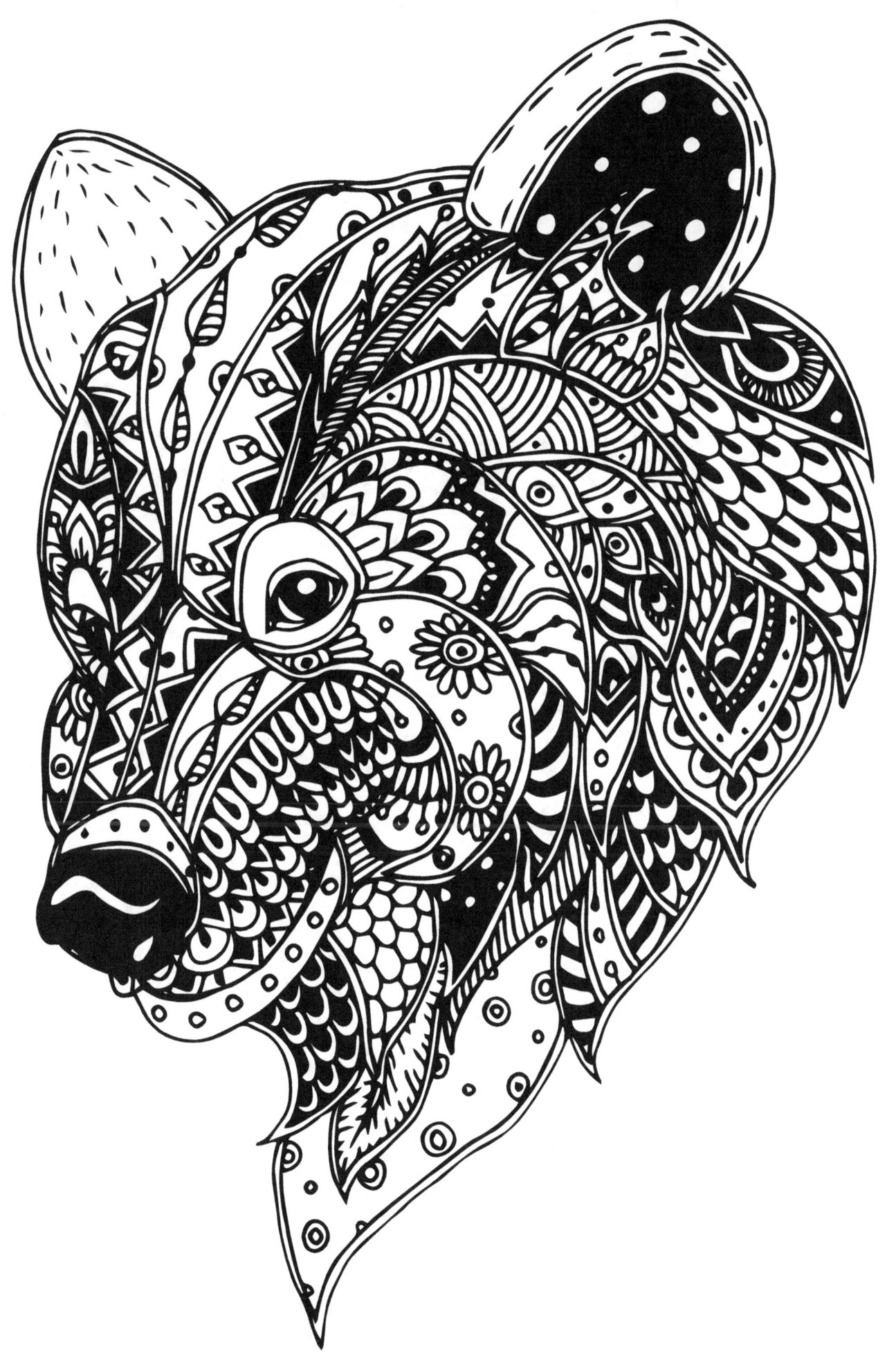

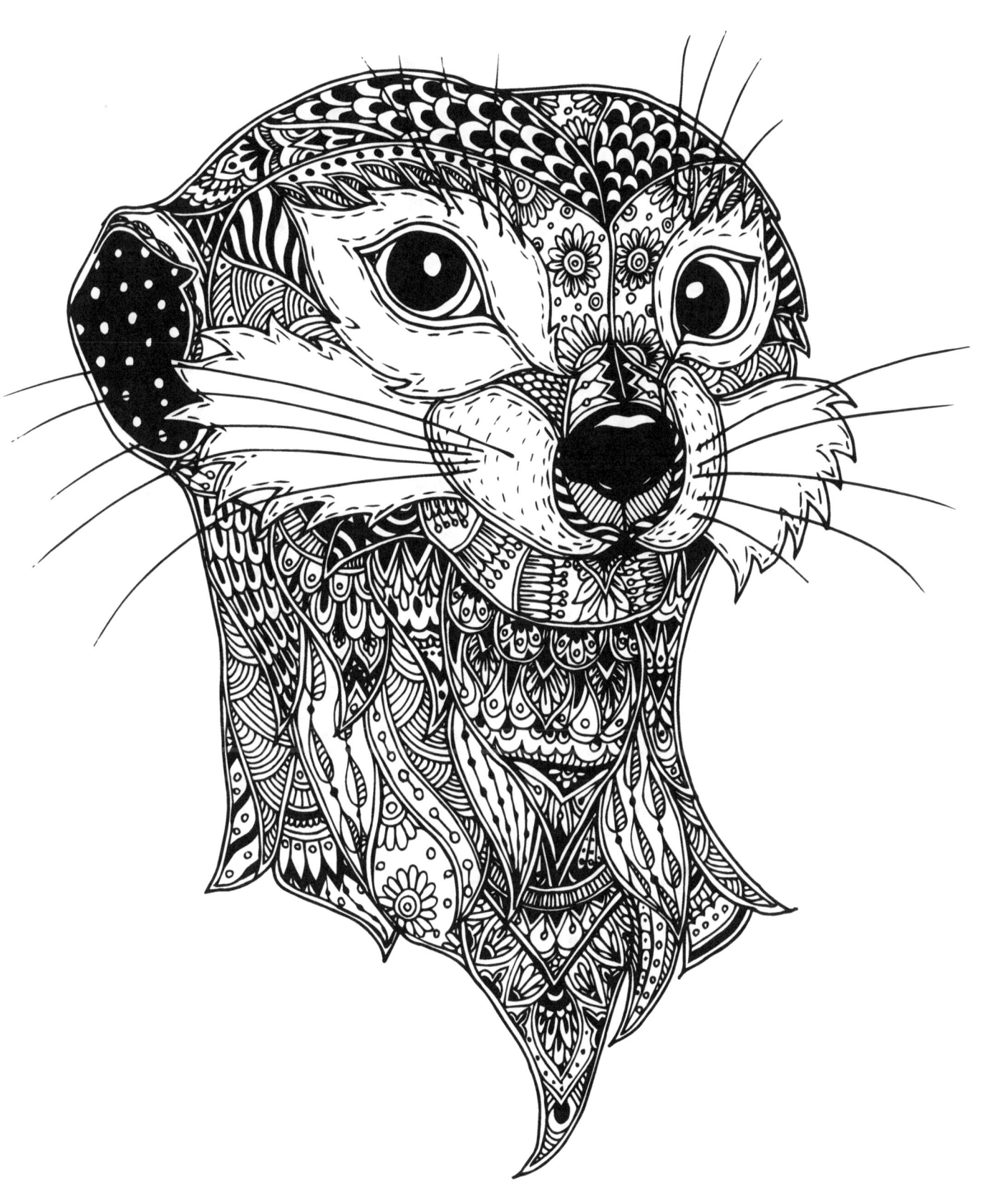

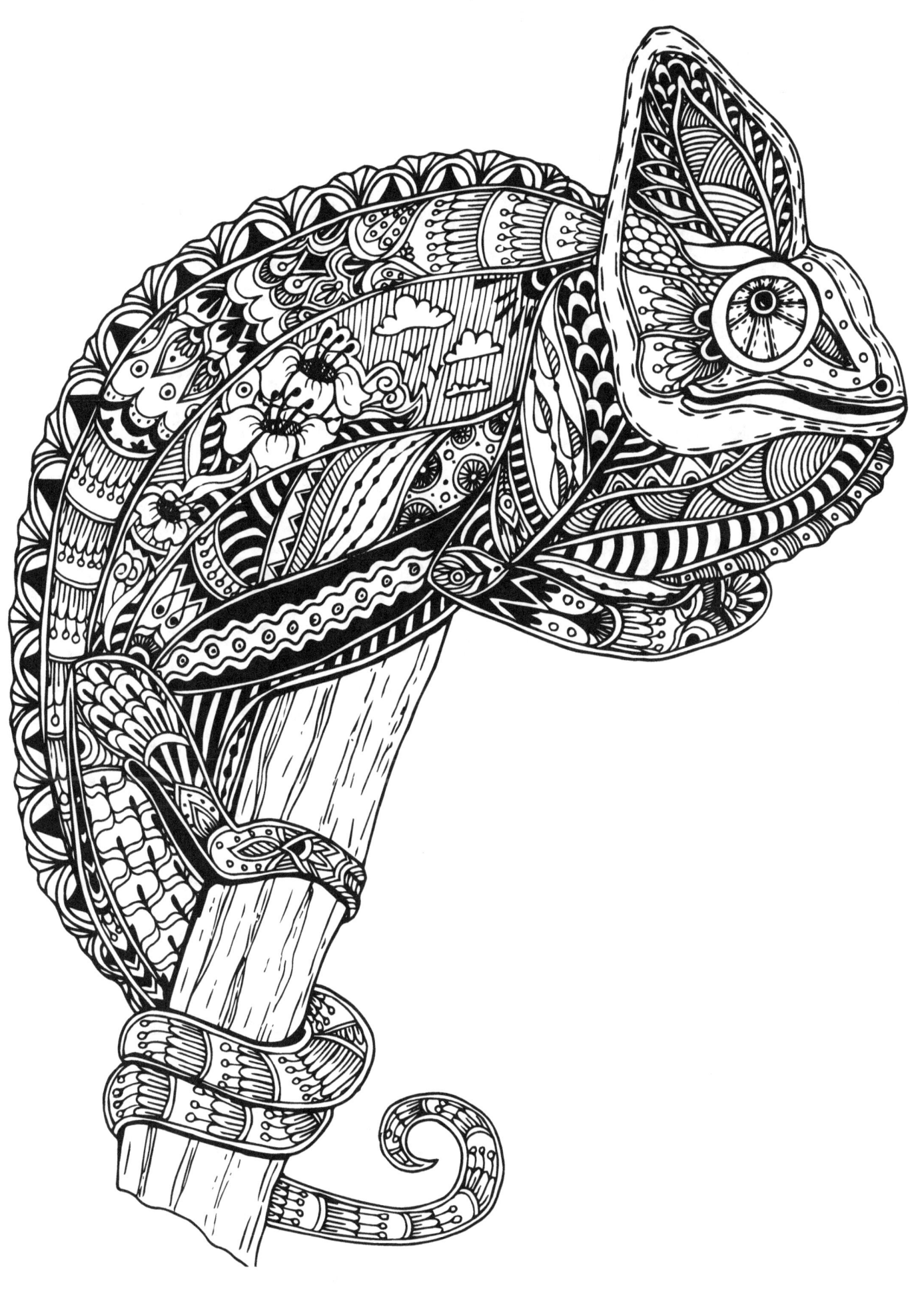

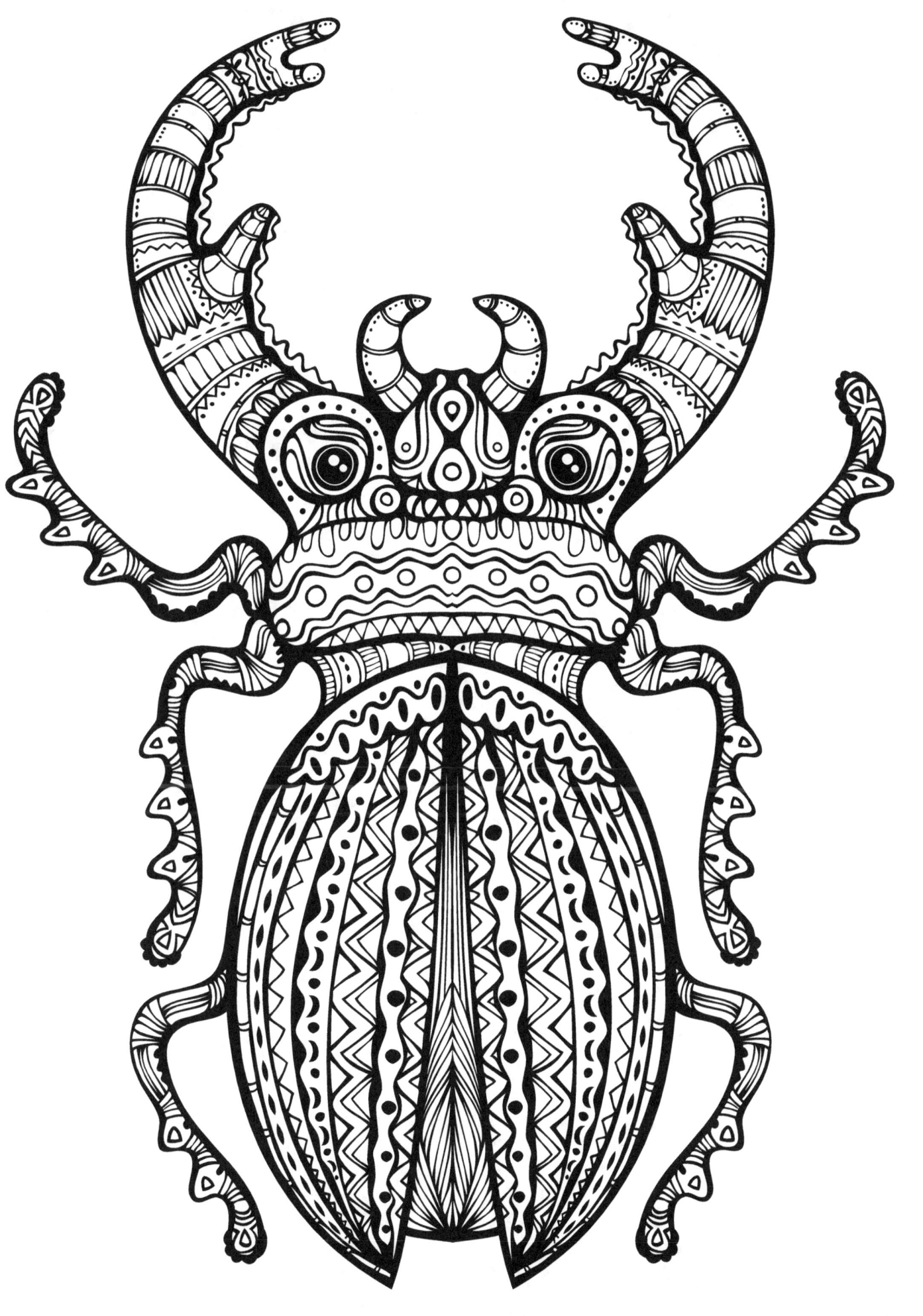

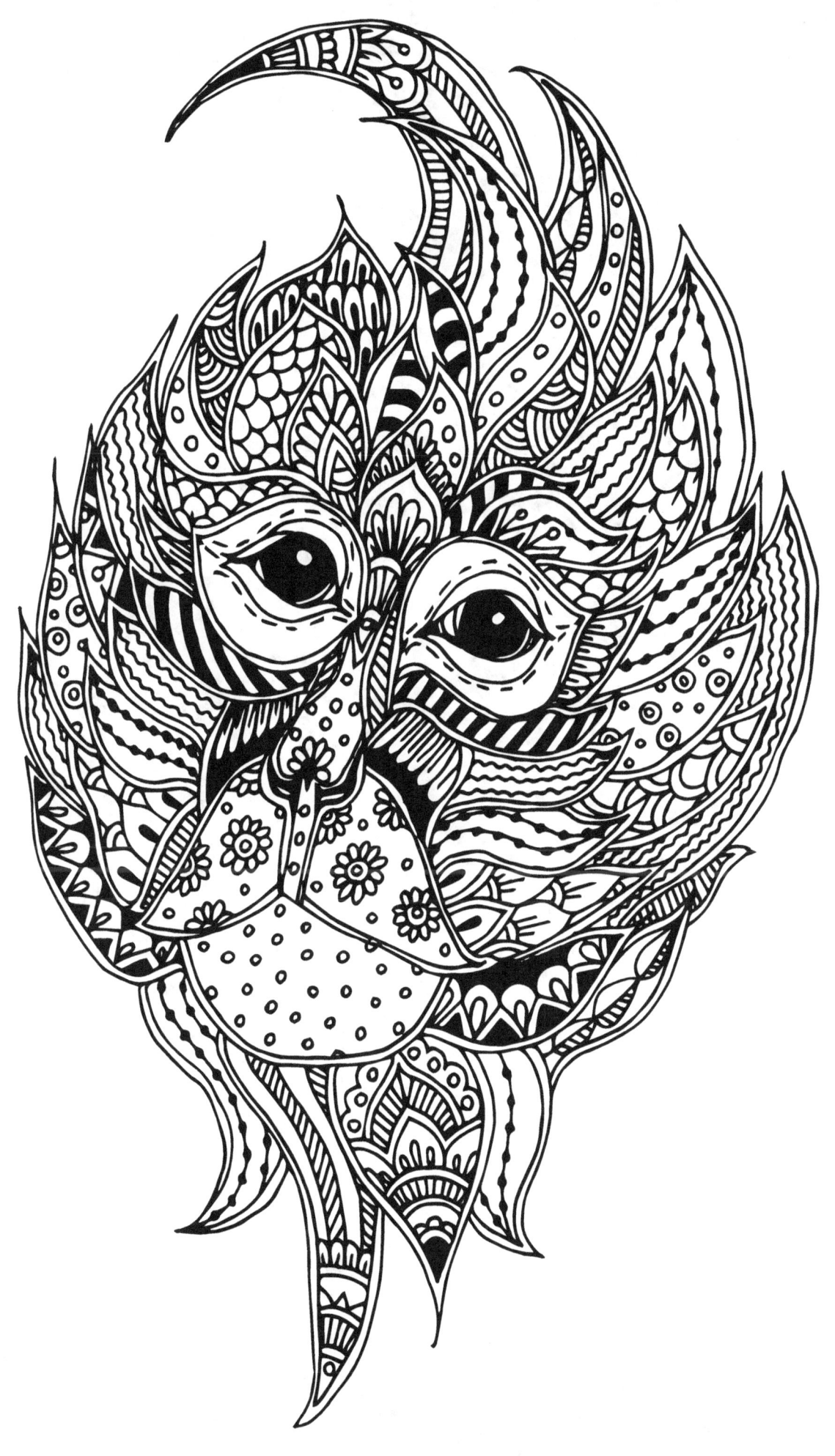

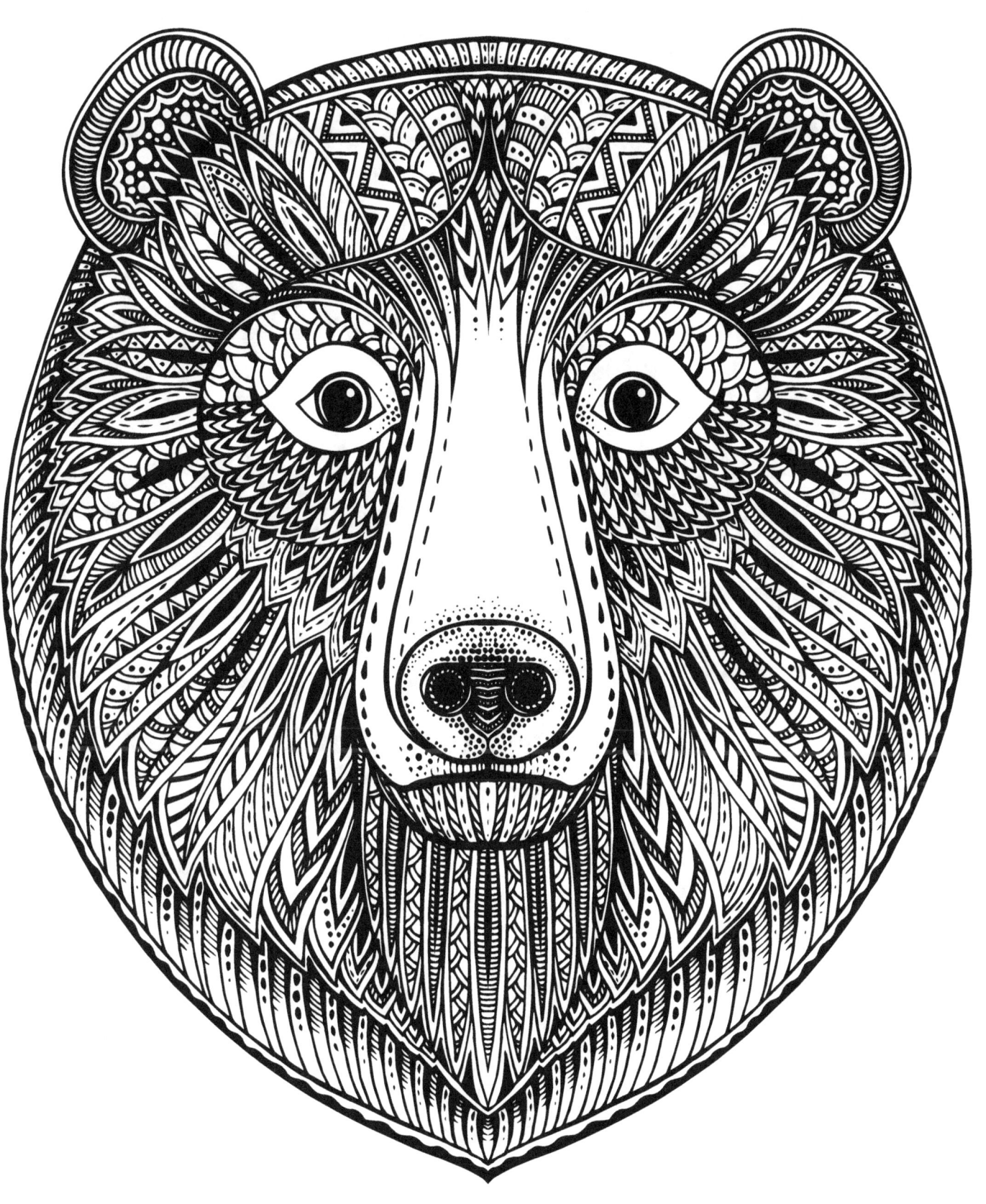

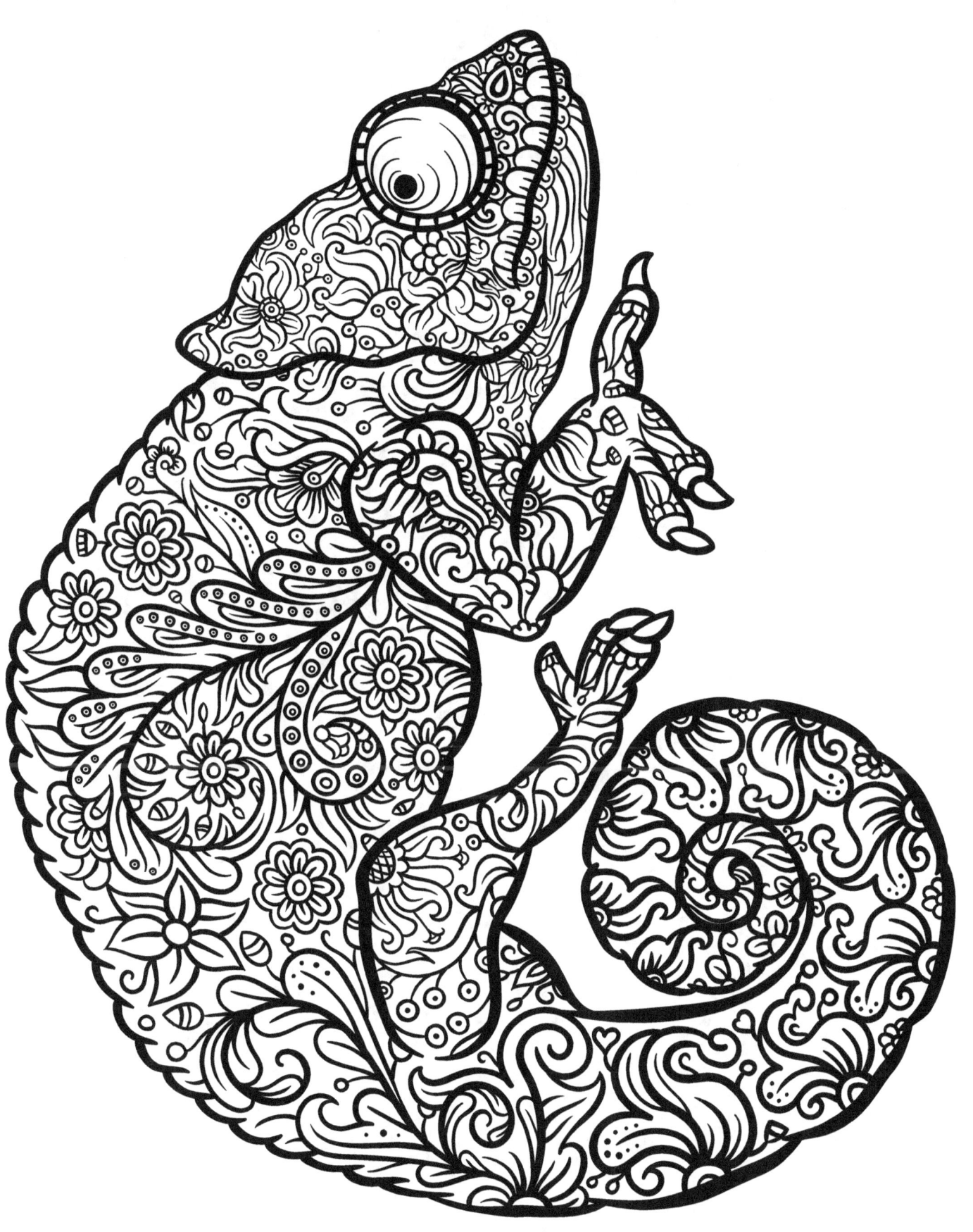

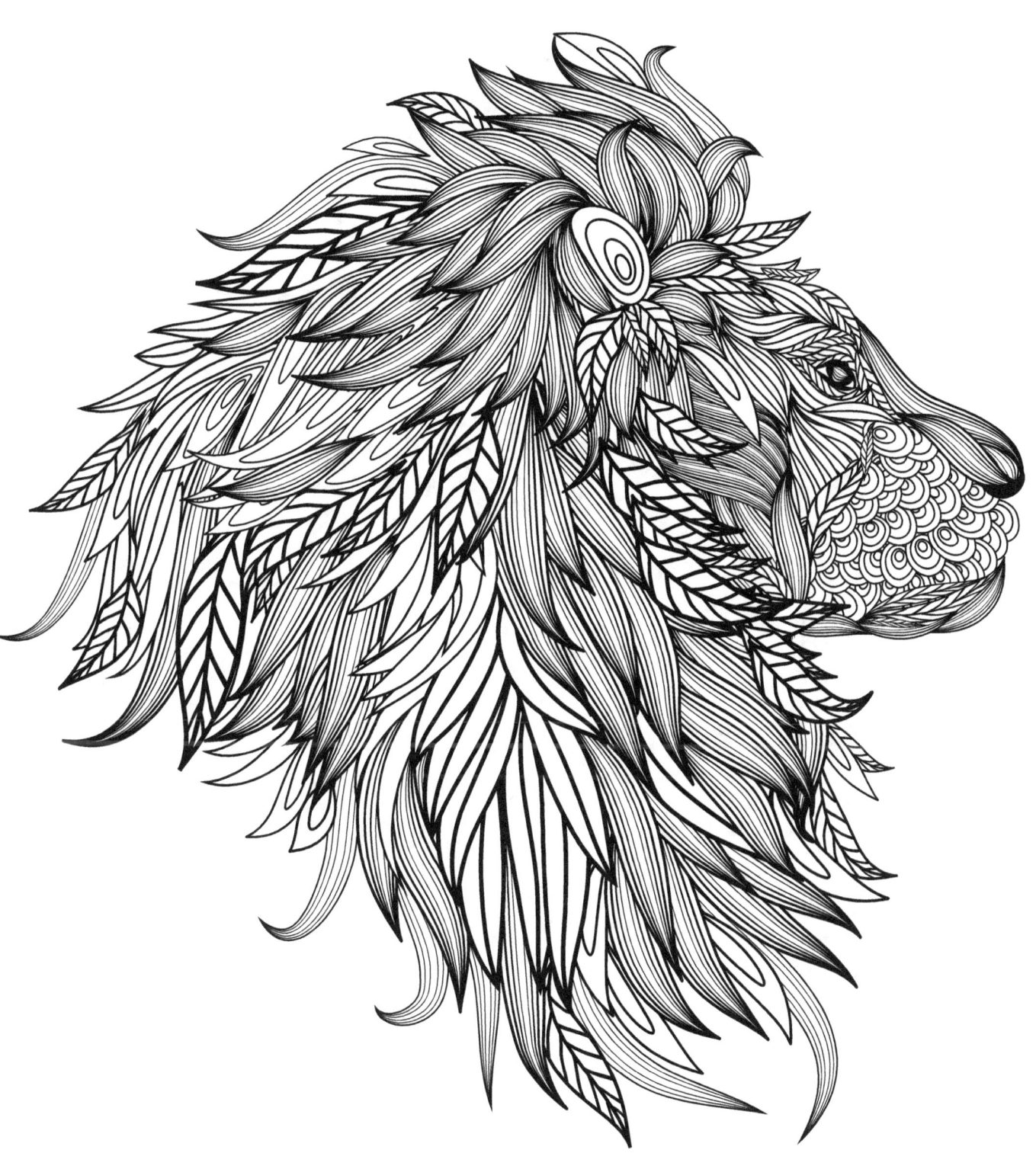

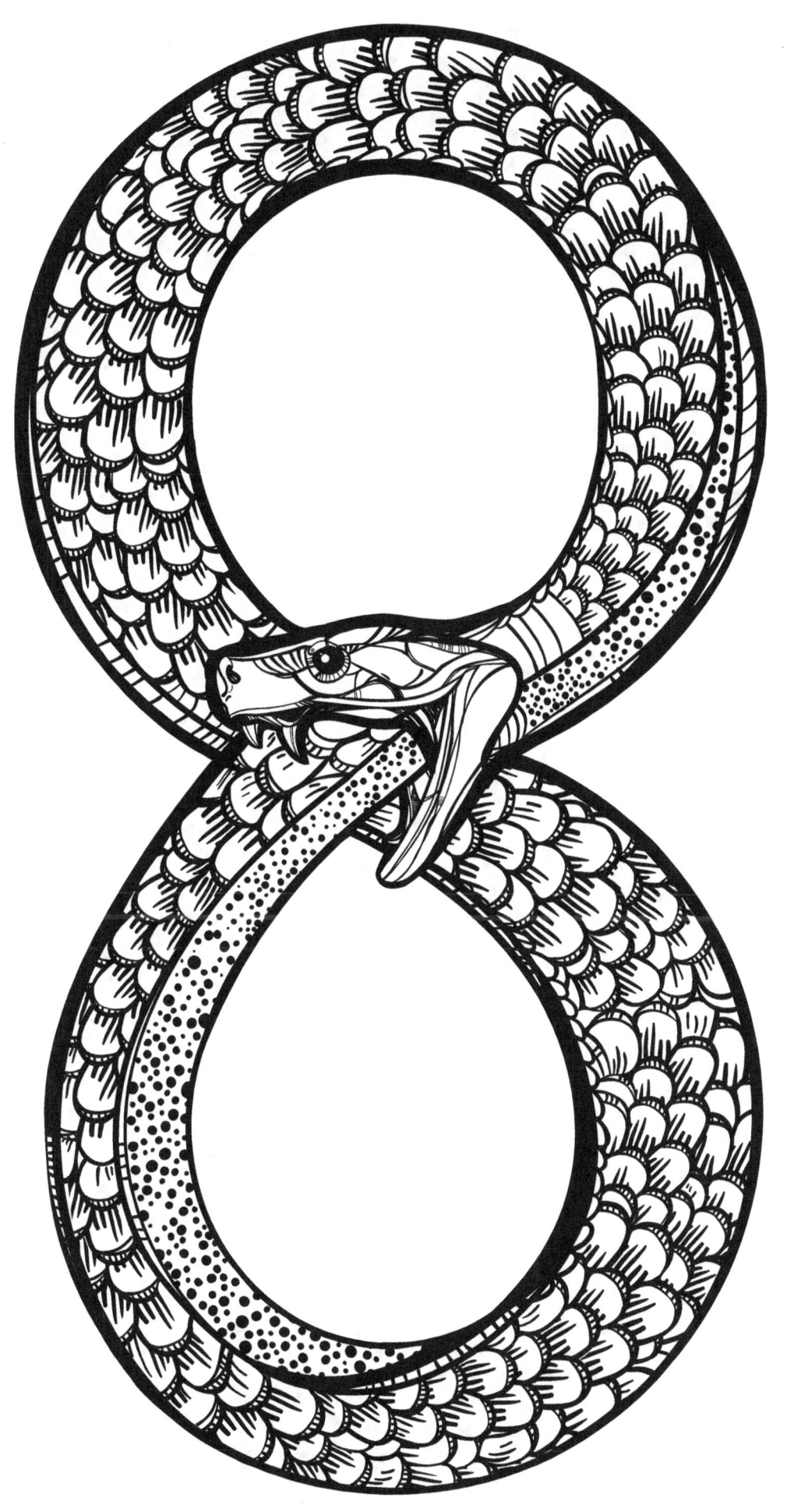

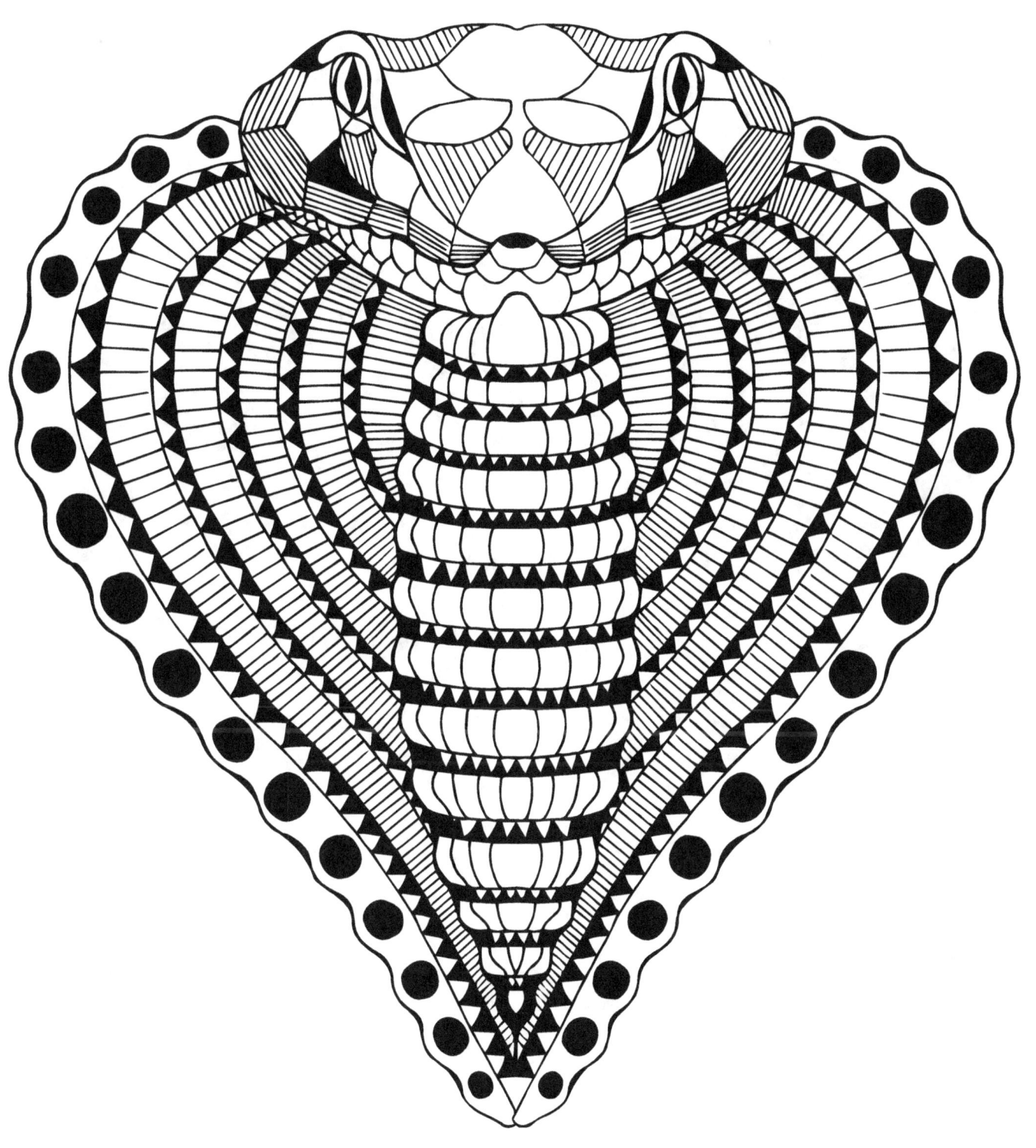

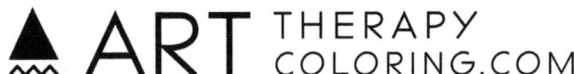

Test Your Colors

Drawings

Drawings

Best Selling Art Therapy Coloring Books

Coloring Books For Adults:

- Zombie Coloring Book: Black Background
- Butterfly Coloring Book For Adults: Black Background
- Tattoo Coloring Book: Black Background
- Coloring Books for Adults Relaxation: Native American Inspired Designs
- Fishing Coloring Book for Adults: Black Background

Coloring Books For Men:

- Coloring Book for Men: Anti-Stress Designs Vol 1
- Coloring Book For Men: Fishing Designs
- Coloring Book For Men: Tattoo Designs
- Coloring Books for Men: Hunting
- Coloring Book For Men: Biker Designs

Coloring Books For Seniors:

- Coloring Book For Seniors: Nature Designs Vol 1
- Coloring Book For Seniors: Anti-Stress Designs Vol 1
- Coloring Books for Seniors: Relaxing Designs
- Coloring Book For Seniors: Floral Designs Vol 1
- Coloring Book For Seniors: Ocean Designs Vol 1

Coloring Books For Teens and Tweens:

- Coloring Books For Teens: Ocean Designs
- Coloring Books for Teen Girls Vol 1
- Teen Inspirational Coloring Books
- Coloring Book for Teens: Anti-Stress Designs Vol 1
- Tween Coloring Books For Girls: Cute Animals

Coloring Books For Older Kids:

- Coloring Books For Girls: Cute Animals
- Horse Coloring Book For Girls
- Coloring Books For Boys: Sharks
- Coloring Books for Boys: Animal Designs
- Unicorn Coloring Book for Girls
- Detailed Coloring Books For Kids

Art Therapy Coloring Books

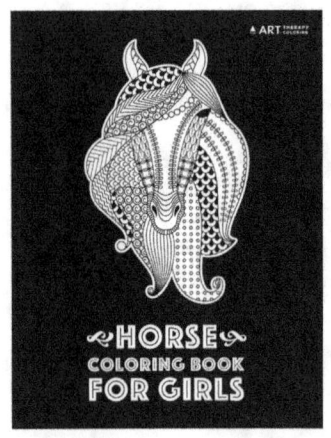

HORSE
COLORING BOOK
FOR GIRLS

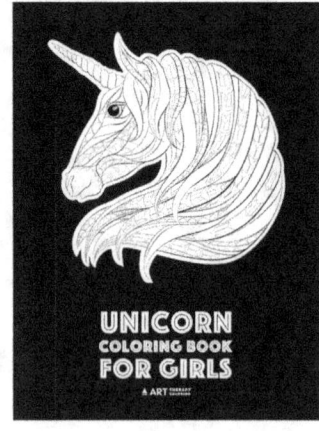

UNICORN
COLORING BOOK
FOR GIRLS

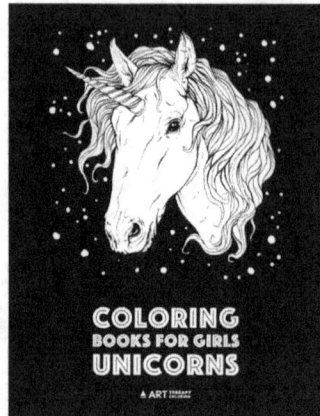

COLORING
BOOKS FOR GIRLS
UNICORNS

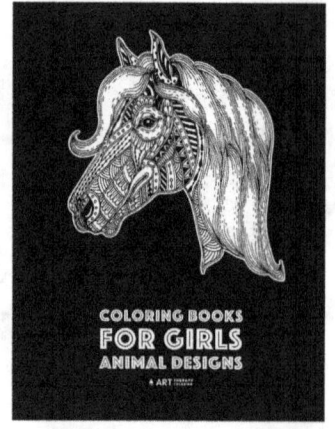

COLORING BOOKS
FOR GIRLS
ANIMAL DESIGNS

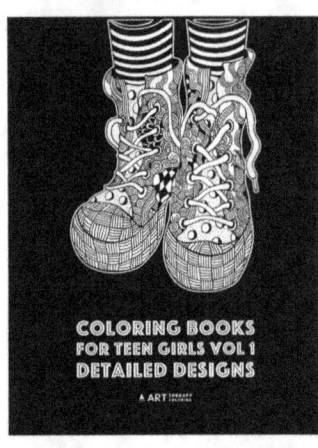

COLORING BOOKS
FOR TEEN GIRLS VOL 1
DETAILED DESIGNS

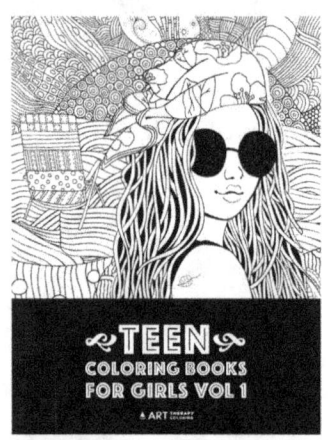

TEEN
COLORING BOOKS
FOR GIRLS VOL 1

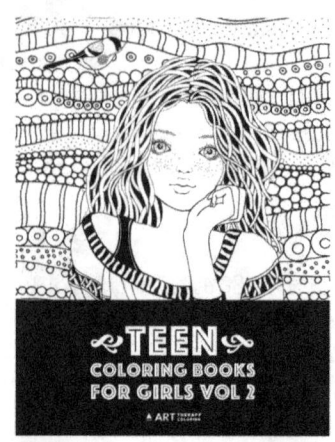

TEEN
COLORING BOOKS
FOR GIRLS VOL 2

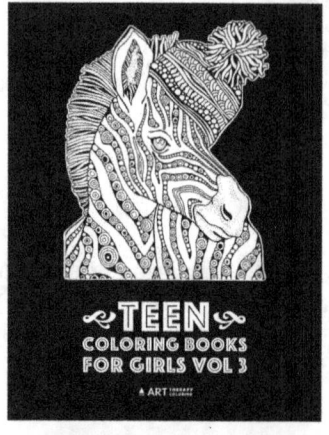

TEEN
COLORING BOOKS
FOR GIRLS VOL 3

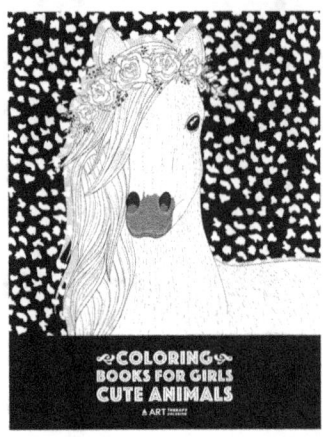

COLORING
BOOKS FOR GIRLS
CUTE ANIMALS

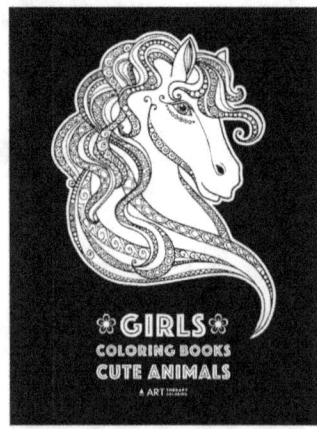

GIRLS
COLORING BOOKS
CUTE ANIMALS

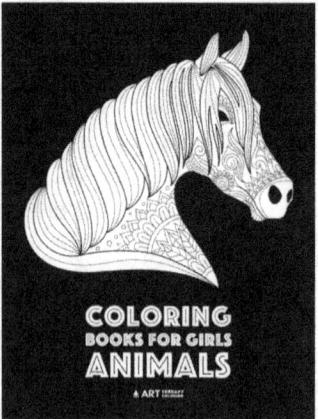

COLORING
BOOKS FOR GIRLS
ANIMALS

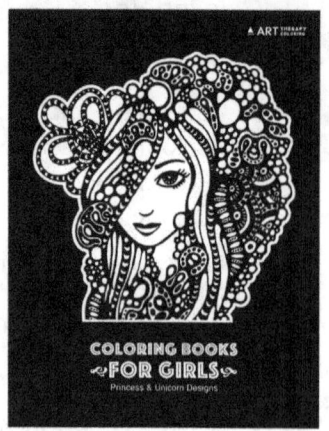

COLORING BOOKS
FOR GIRLS
Princess & Unicorn Designs

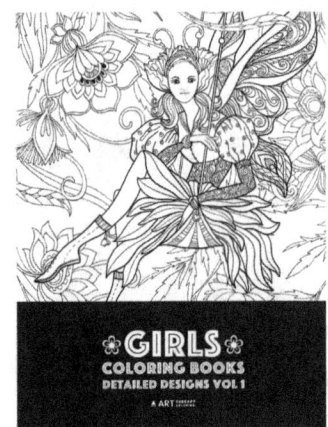

GIRLS
COLORING BOOKS
DETAILED DESIGNS VOL 1

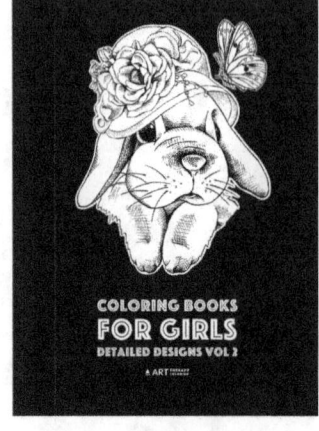

COLORING BOOKS
FOR GIRLS
DETAILED DESIGNS VOL 2

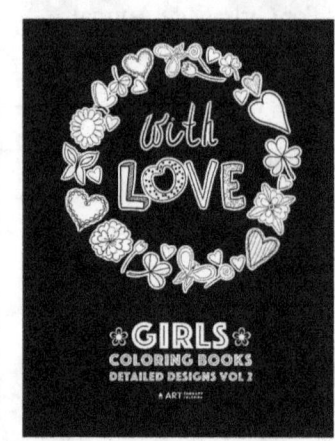

GIRLS
COLORING BOOKS
DETAILED DESIGNS VOL 2

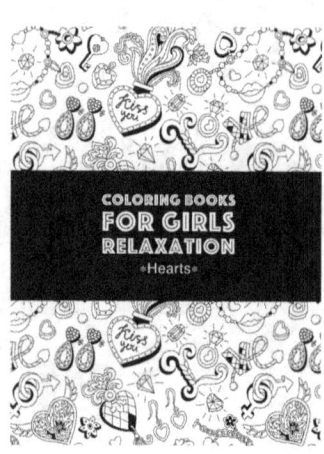

COLORING BOOKS
FOR GIRLS
RELAXATION
Hearts

Art Therapy Coloring Books

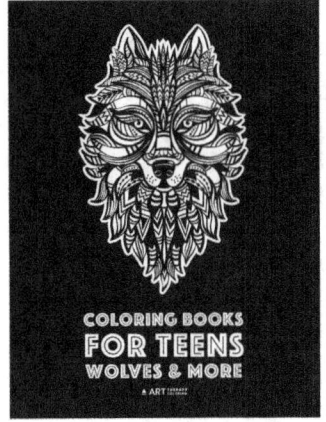

COLORING BOOKS
FOR TEENS
WOLVES & MORE

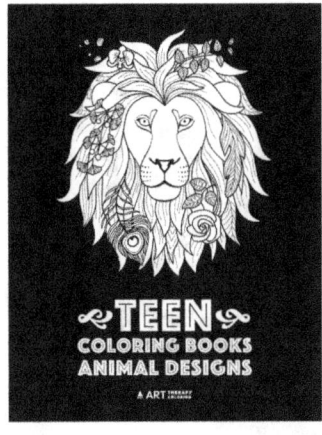

~TEEN~
COLORING BOOKS
ANIMAL DESIGNS

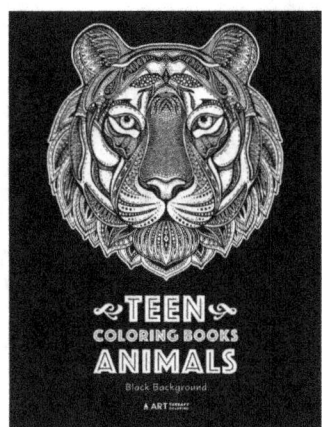

~TEEN~
COLORING BOOKS
ANIMALS
Black Background

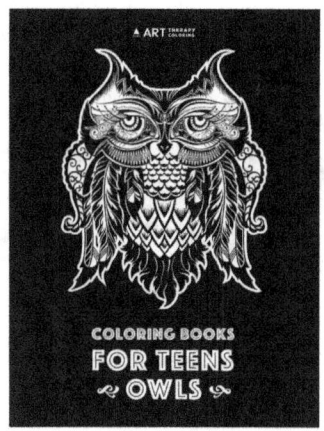

COLORING BOOKS
FOR TEENS
~OWLS~

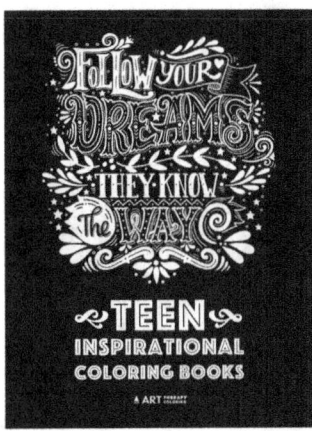

~TEEN~
INSPIRATIONAL
COLORING BOOKS

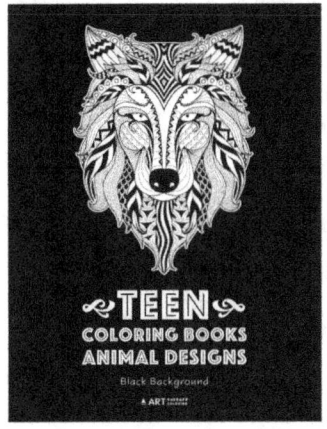

~TEEN~
COLORING BOOKS
ANIMAL DESIGNS
Black Background

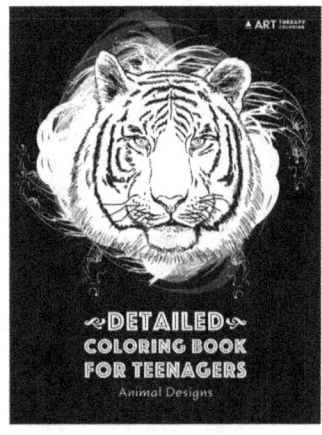

~DETAILED~
COLORING BOOK
FOR TEENAGERS
Animal Designs

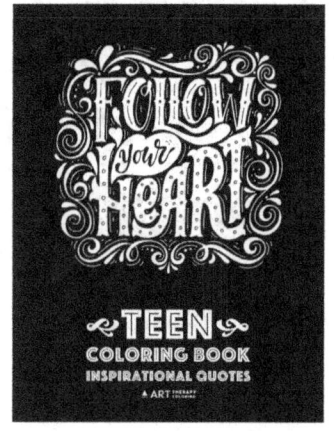

~TEEN~
COLORING BOOK
INSPIRATIONAL QUOTES

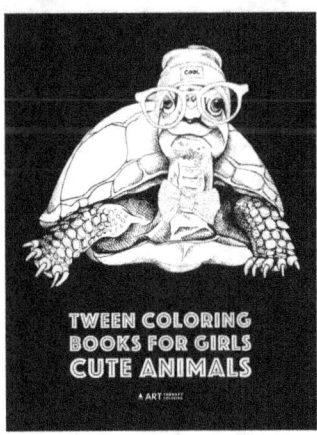

TWEEN COLORING
BOOKS FOR GIRLS
CUTE ANIMALS

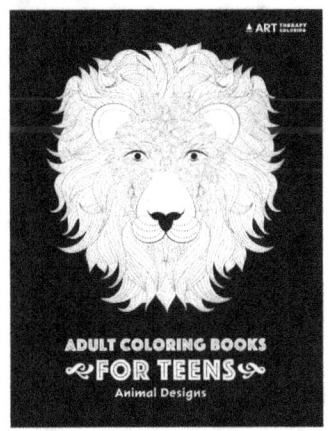

ADULT COLORING BOOKS
~FOR TEENS~
Animal Designs

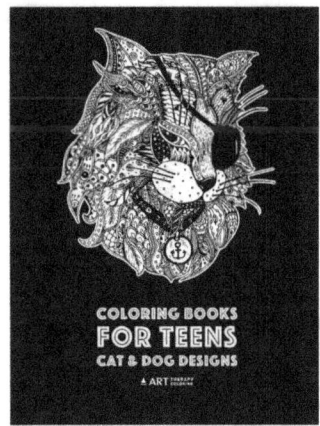

COLORING BOOKS
FOR TEENS
CAT & DOG DESIGNS

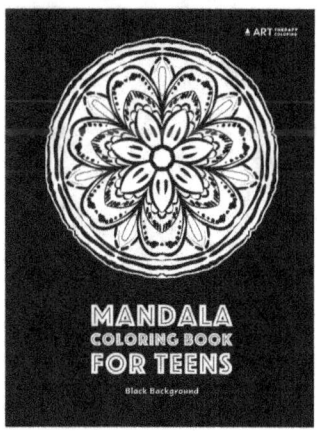

MANDALA
COLORING BOOK
FOR TEENS
Black Background

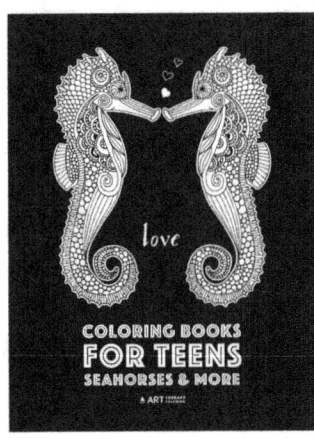

COLORING BOOKS
FOR TEENS
SEAHORSES & MORE

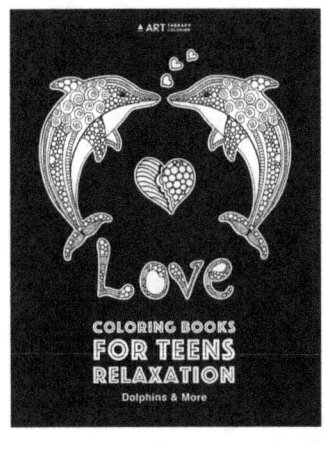

COLORING BOOKS
FOR TEENS
RELAXATION
Dolphins & More

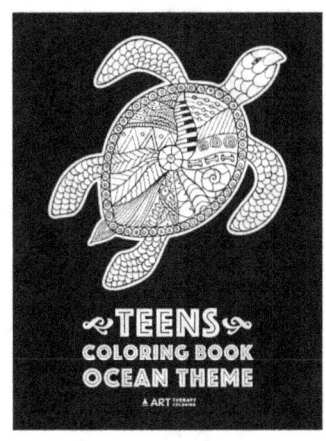

~TEENS~
COLORING BOOK
OCEAN THEME

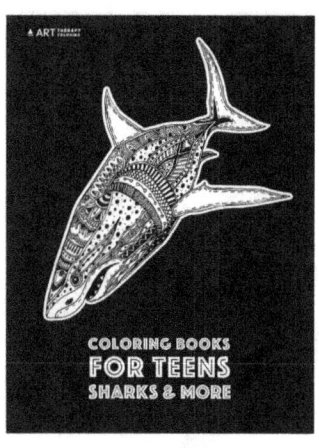

COLORING BOOKS
FOR TEENS
SHARKS & MORE

Art Therapy Coloring Books

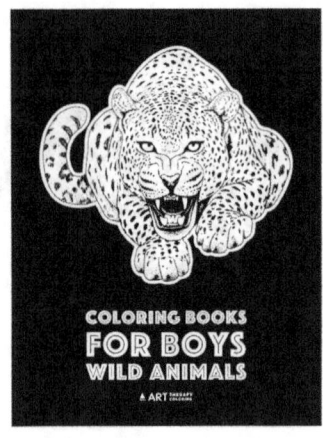

COLORING BOOKS
FOR BOYS
WILD ANIMALS
ART THERAPY COLORING

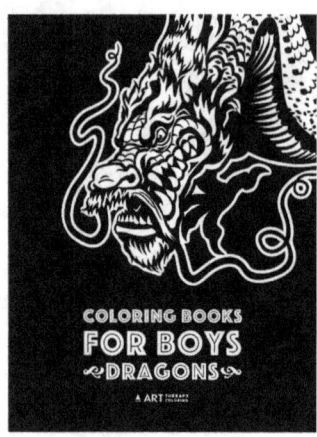

COLORING BOOKS
FOR BOYS
DRAGONS
ART THERAPY COLORING

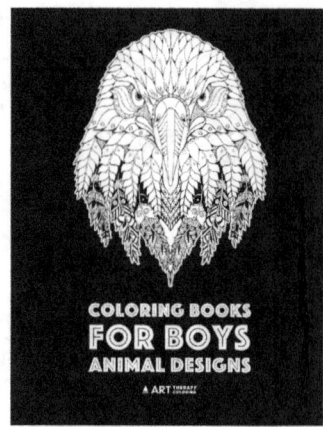

COLORING BOOKS
FOR BOYS
ANIMAL DESIGNS
ART THERAPY COLORING

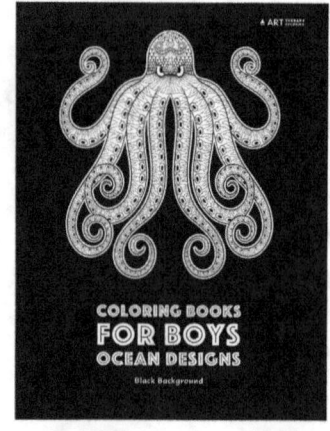

COLORING BOOKS
FOR BOYS
OCEAN DESIGNS
Black Background

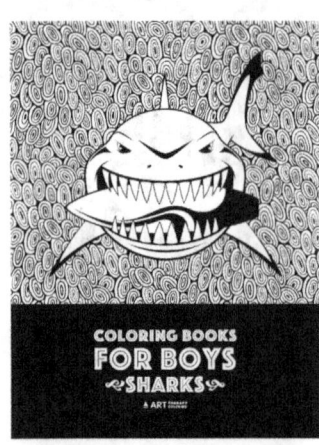

COLORING BOOKS
FOR BOYS
SHARKS
ART THERAPY COLORING

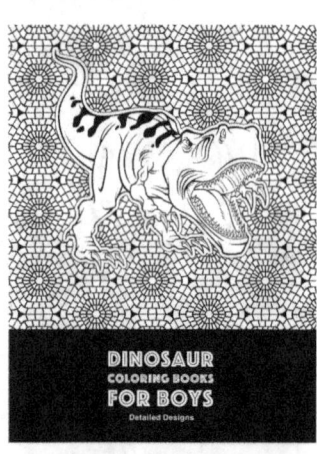

DINOSAUR
COLORING BOOKS
FOR BOYS
Detailed Designs

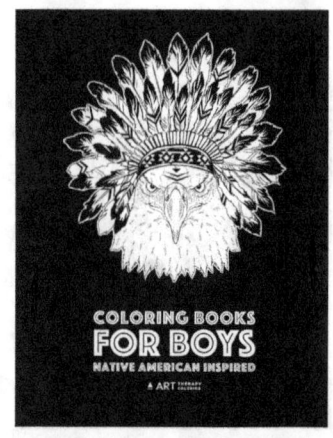

COLORING BOOKS
FOR BOYS
NATIVE AMERICAN INSPIRED
ART THERAPY COLORING

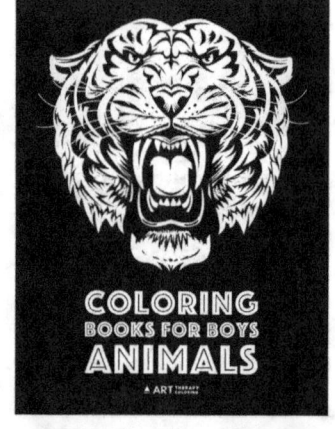

COLORING
BOOKS FOR BOYS
ANIMALS
ART THERAPY COLORING

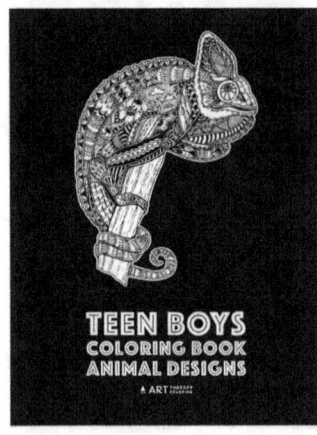

TEEN BOYS
COLORING BOOK
ANIMAL DESIGNS
ART THERAPY COLORING

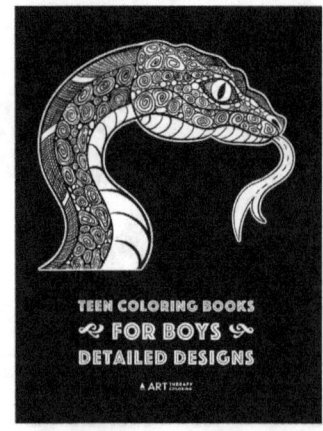

TEEN COLORING BOOKS
FOR BOYS
DETAILED DESIGNS
ART THERAPY COLORING

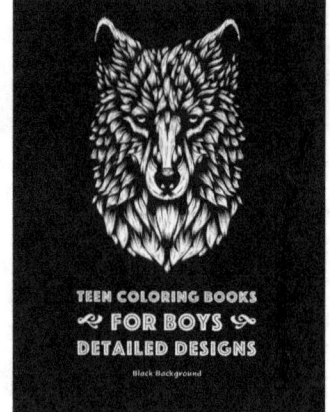

TEEN COLORING BOOKS
FOR BOYS
DETAILED DESIGNS
Black Background

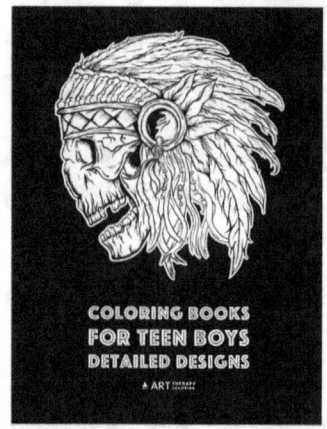

COLORING BOOKS
FOR TEEN BOYS
DETAILED DESIGNS
ART THERAPY COLORING

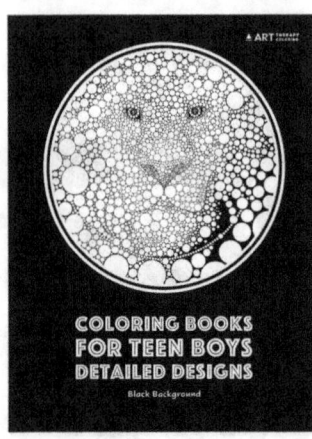

COLORING BOOKS
FOR TEEN BOYS
DETAILED DESIGNS
Black Background

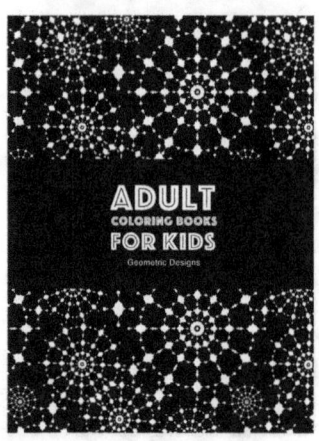

ADULT
COLORING BOOKS
FOR KIDS
Geometric Designs

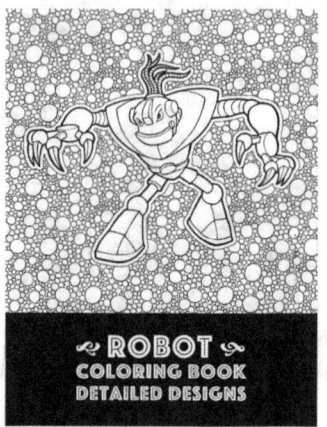

ROBOT
COLORING BOOK
DETAILED DESIGNS

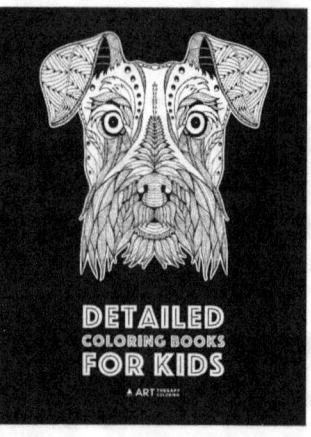

DETAILED
COLORING BOOKS
FOR KIDS
ART THERAPY COLORING

Art Therapy Coloring Books

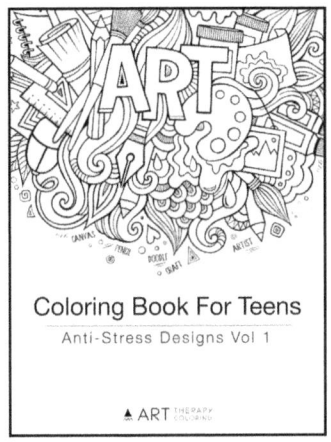

Coloring Book For Teens
Anti-Stress Designs Vol 1

ART THERAPY COLORING

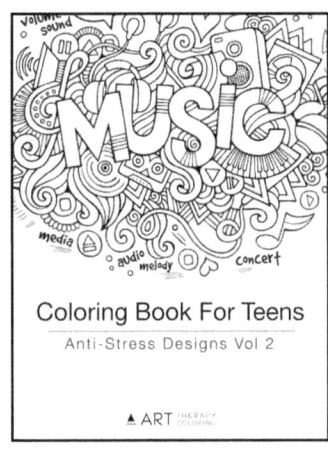

Coloring Book For Teens
Anti-Stress Designs Vol 2

ART THERAPY COLORING

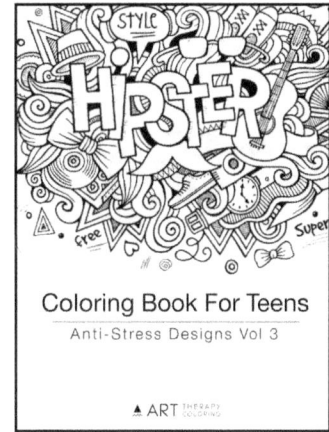

Coloring Book For Teens
Anti-Stress Designs Vol 3

ART THERAPY COLORING

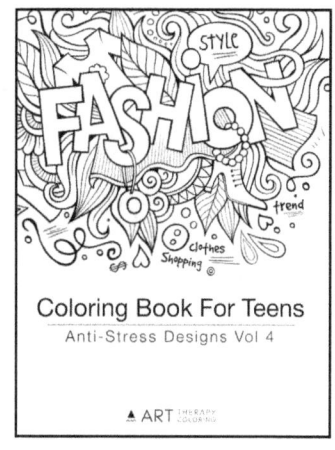

Coloring Book For Teens
Anti-Stress Designs Vol 4

ART THERAPY COLORING

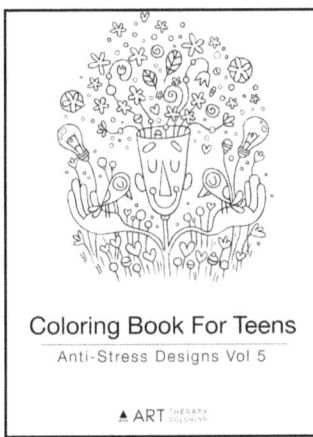

Coloring Book For Teens
Anti-Stress Designs Vol 5

ART THERAPY COLORING

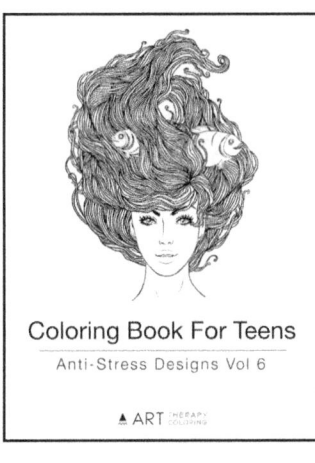

Coloring Book For Teens
Anti-Stress Designs Vol 6

ART THERAPY COLORING

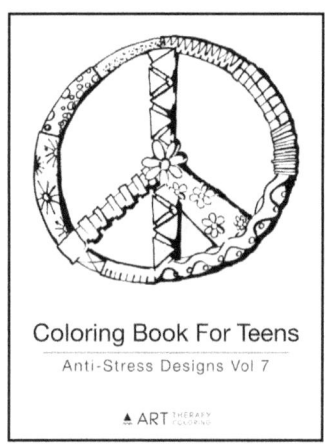

Coloring Book For Teens
Anti-Stress Designs Vol 7

ART THERAPY COLORING

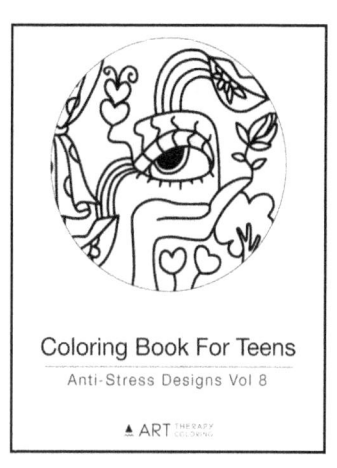

Coloring Book For Teens
Anti-Stress Designs Vol 8

ART THERAPY COLORING

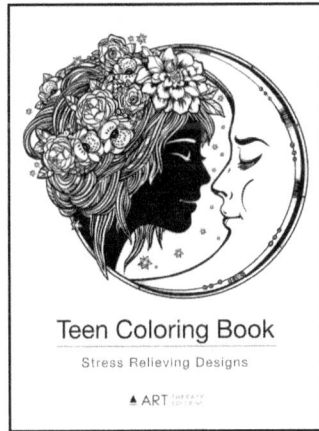

Teen Coloring Book
Stress Relieving Designs

ART THERAPY COLORING

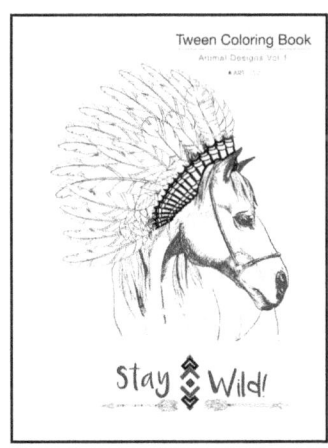

Tween Coloring Book
Animal Designs Vol 1

Stay Wild!

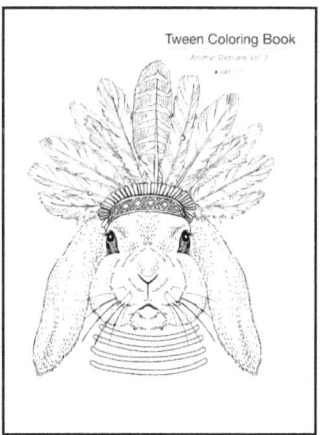

Tween Coloring Book
Animal Designs Vol 2

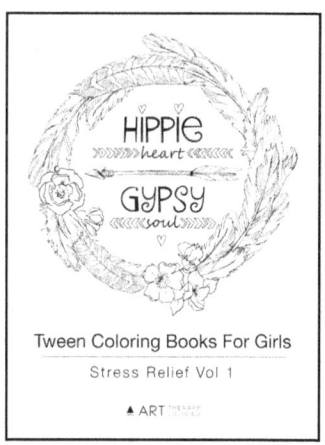

Tween Coloring Books For Girls
Stress Relief Vol 1

ART THERAPY COLORING

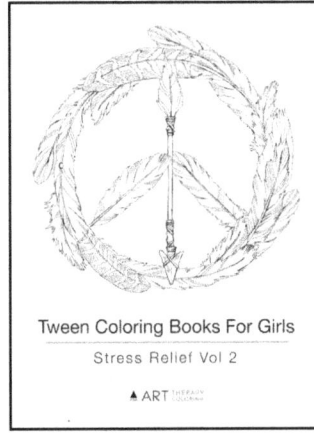

Tween Coloring Books For Girls
Stress Relief Vol 2

ART THERAPY COLORING

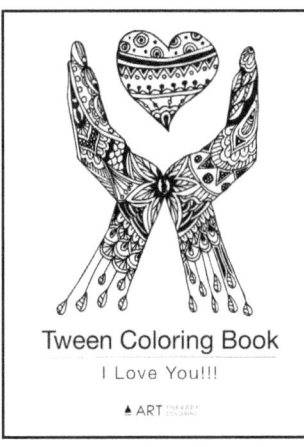

Tween Coloring Book
I Love You!!!

ART THERAPY COLORING

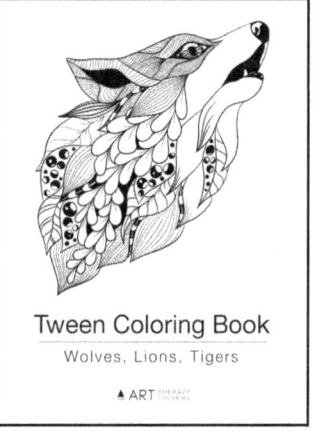

Tween Coloring Book
Wolves, Lions, Tigers

ART THERAPY COLORING

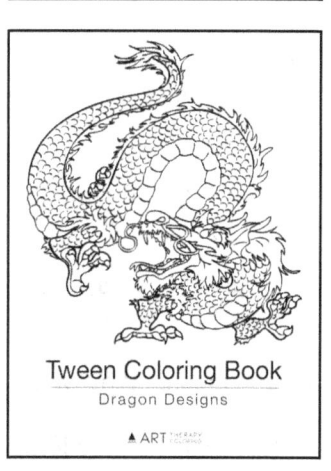

Tween Coloring Book
Dragon Designs

ART THERAPY COLORING

Teen Boys Coloring Book
Animal Designs

Published by:
Art Therapy Coloring
www.arttherapycoloring.com

Images Licensed by Shutterstock

ISBN: 978-1-64126-028-2